Sayyidah Fāṭimah عليها السلام An Exemplar for Mankind

Āyatullāh Jawādī Āmulī

AL-BURĀQ

Copyright

ISBN: 978-1-956276-52-7
Printed and published by al-Burāq Publications.
Translated and annotated by al-Burāq Publications. Where needed, context and transliterations were added. Some minor edits were made to the translated text.

Ordering Information
We offer discounts and promotions for wholesale purchases, non-profit organizations, and other educational institutions. Contact us at the email below for further information.

www.al-Buraq.org
publications@al-Buraq.org

First Edition | July 2024

Dedication

The publication of this book was made possible through the generous support of our donors.

Please recite *Sūrat al-Fātiḥah* and ask God for the Divine reward (*thawāb*) to be conferred upon the donors and also the souls of all the deceased in whose memory their loved ones have contributed graciously towards the publication of *Sayyidah Fāṭimah* عليها السلام*: An Exemplar for Mankind*.

We begin by giving all praise and thanks to God for giving us the *tawfīq* to translate this book. He has guided us and without Him, we would not have been guided to the straight path embodied by the Prophet Muḥammad and the Ahl al-Bayt.

This book is dedicated to all the scholars, martyrs and believers who worked tirelessly to promote the pure Muḥammadan path.

We want to also give our thanks and appreciation to all believers from around the world and acknowledge the team which helped al-Burāq Publications complete this work, spending countless hours to make its publication possible. Please recite Sūrat al-Fātiḥah on behalf of them, their families, and their marḥūmīn.

This book is dedicated in honor of the following individuals. Please remember them in your prayers and may God have mercy on them and their loved ones.

Sakina Fatima Husain and Haider Ali Husain
kindly request that you please recite
Sūrat al-Fātiḥah
for their great grandparents

Basharat Husain son of Shujat Husain &
Kishwari Fatima daughter of Momin Husain

Akhtar Husain son of Mohammad Amil &
Kaneez Fatima daughter of Haider Husain

Syed Akhtar Abbas Naqvi son of Syed Nayyar Hussain Naqvi &
Syeda Tahera Abbas Naqvi daughter of Syed Hadi Hussain Naqvi

Syed Shakir Hussain Zaidi son of Syed Mumtaz Zaidi

We hope that you take the time to read this book to increase your connection to God ﷻ, the Prophet ﷺ, and his Ahl al-Bayt عليهم السلام

Dr. Azmat & Sarah Husain

Duʿāʾ al-Ḥujjah

اللّهُمَّ كُنْ لِوَلِيِّكَ الْحُجَّةِ بْنِ الْحَسَنِ صَلَواتُكَ
عَلَيْهِ وَعَلى آبائِهِ في هذِهِ السّاعَةِ وَفي كُلِّ
ساعَةٍ وَلِيّاً وَحافِظاً وَقائِداً وَناصِراً وَدَليلاً
وَعَيْناً حَتّى تُسْكِنَهُ أَرْضَكَ طَوْعاً وَتُمَتِّعَهُ فيها طَويلاً

O God, be, for Your representative, the Ḥujjat (proof), son of al-Ḥasan, Your blessings be upon him and his forefathers, in this hour and in every hour: a guardian, a protector, a leader, a helper, a proof, and an eye - until You make him live on the Earth, in obedience (to You), and cause him to live in it for a long time.

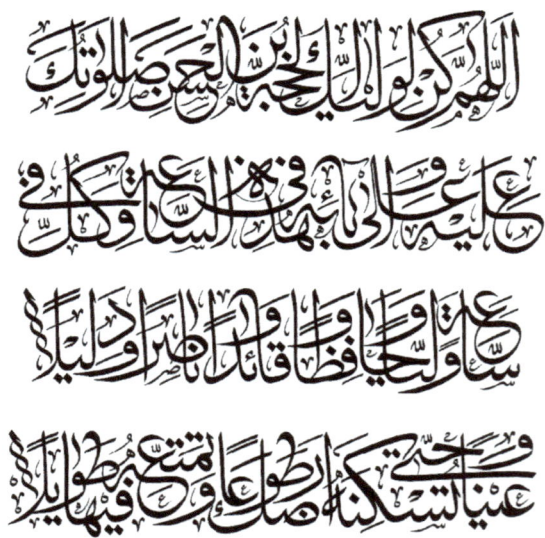

Terms of Respect

The following Arabic phrases have been used throughout this book in their respective places to show the reverence which the noble personalities deserve.

عزّ وجلّ

Used for God, meaning:
Exalted and Sublime (Perfect) is He

صلى الله عليه وآله

Used for Prophet Muḥammad, meaning:
Blessings from God be upon him and his family

عليه السلام

Used for a man (singular) of a high status, meaning:
Peace be upon him

عليها السلام

Used for a woman (singular) of a high status, meaning:
Peace be upon her

عليهما السلام

Used for men/women (dual) of a high status, meaning:
Peace be upon them both

عليهم السلام

Used for men and/or women (plural) of a high status, meaning:
Peace be upon them all

عجّل الله تعالى فرجه الشريف

Used for Imām Muḥammad al-Mahdī, meaning:
May God hasten his return

قدّس سرّه

Used for a deceased scholar, meaning:
May his resting [burial] place remain pure

Transliteration Table

The method of transliteration of Islāmic terminology from the Arabic language has been carried out according to the standard transliteration table below.

ء	ʾ	ر	r	ف	f
ا	a	ز	z	ق	q
ب	b	س	s	ك	k
ت	t	ش	sh	ل	l
ث	th	ص	ṣ	م	m
ج	j	ض	ḍ	ن	n
ح	ḥ	ط	ṭ	و	w
خ	kh	ظ	ẓ	هـ	h
د	d	ع	ʿ	ي	y
ذ	dh	غ	gh		
Long Vowels					
ا	ā	و	ū	ي	ī
Short Vowels					
ـَـ	a	ـُـ	u	ـِـ	i

Table of Contents

Publisher's Forward

بسم الله الرحمن الرحيم

In the Name of God, the Beneficent, the Merciful

Without a doubt, discerning the essence and reality of things is challenging, and this task is even more complex when it comes to understanding the truth about human beings. When this endeavor extends to the most superior and perfect entities of existence, it becomes immeasurable by any means.

When the Prophet Muḥammad ﷺ bestowed upon his daughter عليها السلام the title of *Sayyidah Nisā' al-'Ālamīn*[1], a divine honor, it becomes clear that the only way to truly acknowledge her stature is by admitting our inability to do so fully. Similarly, God's position in terms of knowledge and worship surpasses all human comprehension and the practices of mystical and revelatory rites. Therefore, one can only express their limitations before Him with the admission:

> "We have not comprehended you as you truly deserve to be known, and we have not revered you as you should be worshipped."[2]

---

[1] Translates to: Mistress of the Women of the Worlds.

[2] Majlisī, 'Allamah Muḥammad Bāqir, *Mir'āt al-'Uqūl fī Sharḥ Akhbār Āl al-Rasūl*, Vol. 12, p. 155.

Such a declaration demonstrates a profound understanding of these sacred entities, who embody a fragment of the Universal Creator ﷻ and deserve comparable admiration and praise. However, the existence of these celestial figures among earthly beings enhances the marvel of this occurrence, similar to the truth of the Noble Qur'ān. It resides in the hands of God ﷻ on one side and in the hands of His creations on the other. How can such a profound truth be measured by the standard it transcends? Moreover, what benchmark is capable of assessing such divine creations?

Among the singular entities and the sole holder of existence stands the paramount reality of Sayyidah Fāṭimah al-Zahrā' ﷺ. God ﷻ has lauded her as the *Kawthar*, bestowed upon her the title of 'the immense blessing,' and directed her father to offer prayers in thankfulness for this heavenly endowment:

﴿إِنَّا أَعطَينَاكَ الكَوثَرَ﴾

﴿'innā 'a'ṭaynāka l-kawthar[a]﴾

﴿فَصَلِّ لِرَبِّكَ وَانحَر﴾

﴿fa-ṣalli li-rabbika wa-nḥar﴾

﴾*Indeed We have given you abundance. So pray to your Lord, and sacrifice [the sacrificial camel]**﴿[3]

The definition and portrayal of a human can only be accomplished by the Creator of the universe or by those who mirror Him in comprehension and deeds, conduct, and actions. Her father esteemed her as the best woman in this world, and she has no parallel across all epochs and eras save for Imām ʿAlī b. Abī Ṭālib ﵇. She was an extension of the Prophet's ﷺ physical being and the essence of his spirit. She was not just the daughter of the Prophet, the spouse of Imām ʿAlī ﵇, or the mother of Imām al-Ḥasan and Imām al-Ḥusayn ﵉ and Sayyidah Zaynab ﵆, but she was the pivotal heart of the Ahl al-Bayt and the immaculate lineage ﵈. She alone was capable of successfully enduring the divine test in the mission assigned by God ﷻ, emerging victorious:

> "Oh one who has been tested by God, who created you [and] before he created you, He tested you."[4]

---

[3] Sūrat al-Kawthar, Verses 1-2.

* Or 'raise your hands.' According to this interpretation, the phrase refers to the raising of the hands to the ears during prayers.

[4] Ṭūsī, Shaykh Muḥammad b. Ḥasan, *Miṣbāḥ al-Mutahajjid wa Silāḥ al-Mutaʿabbid,* Vol. 2, p. 711.

Thus, when we pay our respects to her, we honor her with these titles: aṣ-Ṣadīqatu as-Shahīdah, ar-Raḍīyyatu al-Marḍīyyah, al-Fāḍilatu az-Zakīyyah, al-Ḥawrā' al-Insīyyah, at-Taqīyyatu an-Naqīyyah, al-Muḥaddithatu al-'Ilmīyyah, al-Maḍlūmatu al-Maghṣūbah, and al-Muḍṭahidatu al-Maqhūrah. We then proclaim:

> "The one who brings you joy undoubtedly brings joy to the Prophet ﷺ. The person who offends you certainly offends the Prophet ﷺ. Whoever forms a pact with you has formed a pact with the Prophet ﷺ. Anyone who severs ties with you has severed his ties with the Prophet ﷺ, for you are an extension of his being and a fragment of his soul."

The significant and profound contribution of Sayyidah Fāṭimah ﷺ to the endurance of religion is immense. In the days following the demise of the Prophet ﷺ, as the light of his existence dimmed, a solitary star shimmered in the dusty sky of Islām, keeping hearts yearning with its sad and serene voice - that star was none other than Sayyidah Fāṭimah ﷺ. Amidst challenging times, during the reign of Saqīfah, which coincided with the confinement of Ghadīr, the only sorrow that persisted and echoed was that of the final Prophet's daughter ﷺ. She spoke with unwavering bravery about the religion and its continuity through Imām 'Alī ﷺ, emphasizing his virtue and the lack of legitimacy of others.

Given the commendable character of Sayyidah Fāṭimah 🌸 and her unforgettable role in the most sensitive chapter of Islāmic history, these must remain vibrant and enduring. Therefore, the endeavors of religious and cultural institutions, which draw their inspiration from the profound wellspring of the Noble Qurʾān and the Ahl al-Bayt 🌸, must be accurate in their recognition and identification of this virtuous queen of existence. Āyatullāh Jawādī Āmulī has made significant efforts to portray this celestial figure through diverse and fitting narratives. His contributions will surely resonate throughout history. The Center of Scientific Studies and Research at Isrā has showcased his works by gathering and structuring them to reach individuals of wisdom and dedication. This is done in the hope that they may be capable of acknowledging and emulating such a personality. Lastly, it is hoped that this will assist in identifying and rectifying any erroneous or misleading information that may be present.

Given that Sayyidah Fāṭimah 🌸, akin to her esteemed father, was a terrestrial entity and a paragon for humanity despite possessing divine perfection and virtues. She should be viewed as a model in all aspects of life, theoretically and practically. She should be emulated as a role model, not just perceived as a historical figure that now exists solely in minds and books. For this reason, the book presented is titled *Sayyidah Fāṭimah 🌸: An Exemplar for Mankind*.

In conclusion, Isrāʾ Publications extends its heartfelt gratitude to all the individuals and researchers who contributed their efforts to the creation of this book, particularly the respected scholars Mahdī Āqāyī, Jaʿfar Āryānī, and Muḥammad Ḥasan.

May God ﷻ bestow upon them rewards in this life and the hereafter, the most significant of which is intercession on the Day of Judgement.

Isrā Publications

Recognizing the Ahl al-Bayt عليهم السلام

Adolescence and youth represent the most pivotal and sensitive periods in a person's life. During these stages, the drive to seek guidance and the capacity to transform the soul and progress toward perfection and happiness is far greater than in old age. Valuing these moments can assure a bright future and enduring joy for humanity, while neglect or underestimation can result in irreversible harm. In this era of diverse allurements, numerous enticing forces lie in wait for the youth to pursue experiences and the desire to embrace the delightful aspects of existence. Discerning the path of righteousness from the wrong and understanding the gravitational pull of life play a crucial role in determining their ultimate destination.

During this crucial phase, the optimal sustenance for a young individual and his unblemished spirit is to acquaint himself with the wisdom and virtuous actions of religious seniors, guided by the Prophet ﷺ and the Ahl al-Bayt عليهم السلام. Their words and actions are a lighthouse of guidance and truth on this turbulent journey. The Ahl al-Bayt عليهم السلام, particularly Sayyidah Fāṭimah عليها السلام, have attained infallibility and purity through their endeavors. They are the ideal role models to emulate, providing the utmost benefit to those seeking guidance.

Getting acquainted with the customs of the guiding lights, particularly in one's formative years, cultivates a deep affection and interest for them. This interest is essential for steering them toward the divine path and ensuring everlasting joy. The significance of this affection and interest, and emulating it through the model of the infallible beings ﷺ, is underscored by the fact that God ﷻ tells the Prophet ﷺ:

﴿قُل لا أَسأَلُكُم عَلَيهِ أَجرًا إِلَّا المَوَدَّةَ فِي القُربىٰ ۗ
وَمَن يَقتَرِف حَسَنَةً نَزِد لَهُ فيها حُسنًا ۚ إِنَّ اللَّهَ غَفورٌ شَكورٌ﴾

﴿*qul lā 'as'alukum 'alayhi 'ajran 'illā l-mawaddata fī l-qurbā wa-man yaqtarif ḥasanatan nazid lahū fīhā ḥusnan 'inna llāha ghafūrun shakūr*[un]﴾

﴿Say, *'I do not ask you any reward for it except love of [my] relatives.' Whoever performs a good deed, We shall enhance for him its goodness. Indeed God is Forgiving, Appreciative*﴾[5]

This affection serves as the most clear illustration of a good deed.

In a fleeting moment, the chance disappears, and the investment is gone. If we cherish it and gain wisdom and affection for this Sacred Household ﷺ, we will become accustomed to the lifestyle of these radiant figures, which will bring us joy and happiness in this life and the next.[6]

Conversely, the Ahl al-Bayt ﷺ, as per the verses of the Noble Qur'ān, represents the epitome of infallibility and purity. Being perfect entities, they possess the greatest

---

[5] Sūrat ash-Shūrā, Verse 23.

[6] Āmulī, Āyatullāh 'Abd Allāh Jawādī, *Sarūsh Hidāyat,* Vol. 1, p. 79.

ability to receive divine blessings and have been bestowed with unique privileges. As a result, they have been appointed as God's 🕮 representatives on earth, and the rest of humanity has obligations and responsibilities towards them before God 🕮. Among these responsibilities is the duty to obey them out of recognition, and love for them is one of the most explicit duties prescribed in the Noble Qur'ān. Naturally, other duties towards this Holy Household 🕮 would influence one's fate and happiness. However, anyone who does not genuinely comprehend the stature and magnificence of Ahl al-Bayt 🕮 can never grasp the significance and impact of fulfilling these duties. Therefore, it is essential to recognize and understand these guiding stars and clarify their generative and legislative traits, especially Sayyidah Fāṭimah 🕮.[7] Although truly comprehending these figures may be unattainable, humans may be deemed incapable of doing so, and our descriptions may fall short of doing them justice, discussions about the position of Sayyidah Fāṭimah 🕮 's infallibility will be mentioned, inspired by divine words and religious teachings.

"If saltwater's sip is too grand, just a taste will meet demand."

---

[7] Āmulī, Āyatullāh ʿAbd Allāh Jawādī, *Sarchishmah Andīshah*, Vol. 2, p. 208.

Comprehensive Understanding of the Ahl al-Bayt عليهم السلام

Reflecting upon the verses and traditions, can one thoroughly understand Ahl al-Bayt's عليهم السلام infallibility and purity? Furthermore, who can achieve such understanding, and under what circumstances?

Those who seek a basic understanding of these sacred figures can do so. However, a thorough comprehension surpasses human capabilities when we delve into the following subjects.

God's ﷻ verses, and signs in the universe are of two types: existential (*takwīnī*) and legislative (*tashrī'ī*). Existential signs manifest through the creation of beings, demonstrating the magnificence of God ﷻ and the realities of existence. Many of these truths are beyond the grasp of human intelligence and wisdom. On the other hand, legislative signs are divine utterances in the form of God's ﷻ counsels and directives, most of which can only be comprehended through divine revelation. Human beings are limited in fully comprehending the absolute truth of existential and legislative signs. Just as the Noble Qur'ān, in its original form, represents an existential truth of such magnitude that it surpasses our understanding, and its revealed form is accessible to us as legislation and text, so too is the true knowledge of the perfect human being. The epitome of this is seen in the Prophet Muḥammad ﷺ and his Ahl al-Bayt عليهم السلام, particularly Sayyidah Fāṭimah عليها السلام, whose comprehension is beyond human reach. The Ahl al-Bayt عليهم السلام serve as divine existential signs of God ﷻ and are linked to the existential form of the Noble Qur'ān; they embody divine knowledge, hold the truth, and represent the true essence of the Noble Qur'ān and its laws. They are the personification of the divine verses. Based on this comprehension, they are an assembly of existential and legislative constructs.

Such comprehensiveness in the Ahl al-Bayt ﷺ signifies the objective possession of divine perfections and an awareness of existential truths. In other words, they embody all conceivable perfections that a human can attain, devoid of flaws. This unique status can be discerned from these radiant beings' unwavering journey and path through the Noble Qur'ān. As per the narrations of Islāmic scholars, both Shī'ah and Sunnī, the Prophet ﷺ stated:

> "Indeed I am leaving two things among you, to which if you hold onto, you will never stray. One of these two is greater than the other. [They are] the book of God ﷻ, which is a string hanging from the skies to the earth, and my progeny, who are the Ahl al-Bayt ﷺ. These two shall never separate from each other until they reach me in Heaven at the Pool (of al-Kawthar), so be careful how you treat them after me."[8]

The recipients of this divine message are the successors of the prosperous Islāmic civilization in this world. This

[8] Biṭrīq, Yaḥyā b. Ḥasan, *Al-'Umdat*, p. 73.

al-Tirmidhī, Muḥammad, *Sunan al-Tirmidhī*, Vol. 5, p. 329.

implies no era or group will be excluded from this beneficial guidance.

This all-encompassing will demonstrate the perfect alignment of human creation's perfection and divine precision, indicating that all earth's inhabitants need the guidance and leadership of the Noble Qur'ān and Ahl al-Bayt ﷺ in terms of knowledge and practice until the Day of Judgement. No school of thought will arise until the end of human history unless it embodies a worldview connected to the Noble Qur'ān and the Ahl al-Bayt ﷺ, and the response to this connection could be either positive or negative.[9]

Just as the Noble Qur'ān serves as a comprehensive guide to human happiness, it encompasses all of humanity's needs on their journey.

﴿وَنَزَّلْنَا عَلَيْكَ الْكِتَابَ تِبْيَانًا لِكُلِّ شَيْءٍ وَهُدًى وَرَحْمَةً وَبُشْرَىٰ لِلْمُسْلِمِينَ﴾

﴿*wa-nazzalnā 'alayka l-kitāba tibyānan li-kulli shay'in wa-hudan wa-raḥmatan wa-bushrā li-l-muslimīn*[a]﴾

﴿*We have sent down the Book to you as a clarification of all things and as a guidance and mercy and good news for the* Muslims﴾[10]

---

[9] Āmulī, Āyatullāh 'Abd Allāh Jawādī, *Sarchishmah Andīshah,* Vol. 2, p. 110-111.

[10] Sūrat an-Naḥl, Verse 89.

Its verses are clear, interconnected, and harmonious, with no contradictions: "Verses elucidate other verses."[11] Similarly, the Ahl al-Bayt ﷺ interprets all divine instructions and laws. They do not require human education because they are linked with God's ﷻ everlasting wisdom and nourished by that source in knowledge and action.

Thus, the characteristics and customs of these enlightened individuals no longer contradict each other. They have always been in sync and serve as interpreters and validators for each other. Consequently, one of the most effective ways to understand the Prophet's ﷺ tradition is to consult the teachings of the Ahl al-Bayt ﷺ. Similarly, one of the most reliable methods to recognize Sayyidah Fāṭimah's ﷺ tradition is to refer to the insightful words of the Prophet ﷺ and other members of the Ahl al-Bayt ﷺ.[12]

The life and death of all entities are linked to their inherent essence. Anything resistant to death or decay is, to that degree, everlasting and partakes from the wellspring of eternity. Similarly, anything susceptible to illness and disease cannot escape the ravages of decay or death.

---

[11] Majlisī, ʻAllamah Muḥammad Bāqir, *Biḥār al-Anwār*, Vol. 54, p. 218.

[12] Āmulī, Āyatullāh ʻAbd Allāh Jawādī, *Sarchishmah Andīshah*, Vol. 2, p. 112.

A concept, conviction, or theoretical wisdom will be preserved from decay and death when free from fallacy, ignorance, error, or mistake. Similarly, in behavior and action, or practical wisdom, decay, and death manifest when elements like oppression, ignorance, and exploitation are present. If a book conveys the essence of theoretical and practical wisdom devoid of these flaws and maintains this quality, then such a book will remain eternal. Likewise, if a flawless human being mirrors such a book, his status will be safeguarded from the triggers and elements of illness, deterioration, and the like.

God ﷻ presented the Noble Qur'ān as a book without flaws. He proclaimed the following:

﴿إِنَّ الَّذِينَ كَفَرُوا بِالذِّكْرِ لَمَّا جَاءَهُمْ ۖ وَإِنَّهُ لَكِتَابٌ عَزِيزٌ﴾

﴿*'inna lladhīna kafarū bi-dh-dhikri lammā jā'ahum wa-'innahū la-kitābun 'azīz*[un]﴾

﴿لَا يَأْتِيهِ الْبَاطِلُ مِنْ بَيْنِ يَدَيْهِ وَلَا مِنْ خَلْفِهِ ۖ تَنْزِيلٌ مِنْ حَكِيمٍ حَمِيدٍ﴾

﴿*lā ya'tīhi l-bāṭilu min bayni yadayhi wa-lā min khalfihī tanzīlun min ḥakīmin ḥamīd*[in]﴾

﴾Indeed those who defy the Reminder when it comes to them... *Indeed it is an august Book: falsehood cannot approach it, from before it nor from behind it, a [gradually] sent down [revelation] from One Wise, Laudable﴿*[13]

With the passage of time and the advent of heavy shifts in the foundation of theoretical wisdom and the tenets of practical wisdom, no form of imperfection infiltrates the fundamental theoretical and practical pillars of the Noble Qur'ān. If it did, it would be susceptible to invalidity. Hence, the thoughts and deeds of the perfect beings, namely the Ahl al-Bayt ﷺ and Sayyidah Fāṭimah ﷺ, who are akin to such a book, will remain unshakeable.[14]

Therefore, the infallibility of these luminous entities is substantiated both theoretically and practically, presenting them as equivalent to the Noble Qur'ān, about which God ﷻ says:

﴿إِنَّهُ لَقُرْآنٌ كَرِيمٌ﴾

﴾'innahū la-qur'ānun karīm^un^﴿

---

[13] Sūrat al-Fuṣṣilat, Verses 41-42.

* Ellipsis. The phrase omitted, considering the context, is, 'will face a severe punishment.'

[14] Āmulī, Āyatullāh 'Abd Allāh Jawādī, *Sarchishmah Andīshah,* Vol. 2, p. 119.

﴿فِي كِتَابٍ مَكْنُونٍ﴾

﴿*fī kitābin maknūn*[in]﴾

﴿لَا يَمَسُّهُ إِلَّا الْمُطَهَّرُونَ﴾

﴿*lā yamassuhū ʾillā l-muṭahharūn*[a]﴾

﴿*This is indeed a Noble Qurʾān, in a guarded Book,**—*no one touches it except the pure ones*﴾[15]

So, to come in physical contact with the text of the Noble Qurʾān, one should achieve external purity of the body through wudhū, ghusl, or tayammum. However, to connect with the esoteric nature of the Noble Qurʾān, which is divine knowledge and the wisdom of God ﷻ, one must achieve internal purity of the heart through spiritual development and refinement. According to the widely accepted Ḥadīth ath-Thaqalayn (narration of the two weighty things), there is no separation between the Noble Qurʾān and the Ahl al-Bayt ﷺ, and hence the Ahl al-Bayt ﷺ alike the Noble book is also infallible and understanding their status and esoteric nature is not possible without the purity of one's heart. On the other hand, just as the teachings of the Noble Qurʾān have several dimensions and layers, there are also levels of

[15] Sūrat al-Wāqiʿah, Verses 77-79.

* That is, the Preserved Tablet.

understanding regarding the position of the Ahl al-Bayt ﷺ. Therefore, whoever strives more to achieve internal purity will have more success in connecting and understanding these holy beings.[16]

In light of the above, to truly understand the essence of a perfect human being, one must strive to become a perfect human being. This journey involves aligning oneself with the Noble Qur'ān and entering the fortress of tawḥīd. This process is contingent upon gaining knowledge of the Ahl al-Bayt ﷺ, ultimately leading to becoming a representative of God ﷻ on earth. Given the immense challenge of attaining such a divine status, we have no option but to form an understanding based on our limited comprehension. This understanding, however, is likely to be incomplete and inaccurate. Until we grasp the true essence of these holy beings, we will remain far from the truth. The perfect human, exemplified by Sayyidah Fāṭimah ﷺ, is a manifestation of God ﷻ. It has been said about God ﷻ that:

> "His understanding cannot be satisfied by those who attempt to do so, and the height of intellectual courage cannot appreciate Him."[17]

---

[16] Āmulī, Āyatullāh 'Abd Allāh Jawādī, *Sarchishmah Andīshah*, Vol. 2, p. 119-120.

[17] Sharīf Raḍī, Muḥammad b. al-Ḥusayn, *Nahj al-Balāghah*, Sermon 1.

Hence, the least one can do is rejuvenate their thoughts' righteousness, foster love in their heart, and keep their name alive in memory, body, and soul. A person with such a thirst is the one who attains the Kawthar, quenches their thirsty spirit, illuminates their dimmed sight, renews their depleted strength, and finds success in their endeavors.[18]

---

[18] Āmulī, Āyatullāh 'Abd Allāh Jawādī, *Sarchishmah Andīshah,* Vol. 2, p. 132-136.

Ahl al-Bayt عليهم السلام: Exemplars of Guidance

From a religious perspective, an appropriate and practical role model is essential for humanity to attain happiness and tread the path of enlightenment. This individual, who is well-versed in the journey and has successfully navigated it, possesses the capability to guide others towards their destination. Being infallible and immune to misguidance, this person is none other than Prophet Muḥammad ﷺ. God ﷻ presented this exemplary model and guide, immune from any wrongdoing or errors:

﴿لَقَد كانَ لَكُم في رَسولِ اللَّهِ أُسوَةٌ حَسَنَةٌ﴾

﴿la-qad kāna lakum fī rasūli llāhi ʾuswatun ḥasanatun﴾

﴿In the Apostle of God there is certainly for you a good exemplar﴾[19]

Certainly, after following the esteemed Prophet of Islām ﷺ, God ﷻ introduced his immaculate family as deserving of emulation and obedience:

﴿يا أَيُّهَا الَّذينَ آمَنوا أَطيعُوا اللَّهَ وَأَطيعُوا الرَّسولَ وَأُولِي الأَمرِ مِنكُم﴾

﴿yā-ʾayyuhā lladhīna ʾāmanū ʾaṭīʿū llāha wa-ʾaṭīʿū r-rasūla wa-ʾulī l-ʾamri minkum﴾

---

[19] Sūrat al-Aḥzāb, Verse 21.

﴾O you who have faith! Obey God and obey the Apostle and those vested with authority among you﴿[20]

Exempt from flaws and errors, this family is shielded from contamination and has reached their destination under the light of this divine purity. Consequently, they can guide others:

﴿إِنَّمَا يُرِيدُ اللَّهُ لِيُذْهِبَ عَنكُمُ الرِّجْسَ أَهْلَ الْبَيْتِ وَيُطَهِّرَكُمْ تَطْهِيرًا﴾

﴾'innamā yurīdu llāhu li-yudhhiba 'ankumu r-rijsa 'ahla l-bayti wa-yuṭahhirakum taṭhīran﴿

﴾Indeed God desires to repel all impurity from you, O People of the Household, and purify you with a thorough purification﴿[21]

Acknowledging the imperative of emulating Sayyidah Fāṭimah ﷺ, it suffices to note that in both Shī'ah and Sunnī traditions, various comparisons are drawn between her and her father.

'Ā'ishah declares:

---

[20] Sūrat an-Nisā', Verse 59.

Cf. verse 4:54.

[21] Sūrat al-Aḥzāb, Verse 33.

> "I have not witnessed anyone who resembles the Prophet ﷺ more than Fāṭimah ؑ."[22]

She further states:

> "In terms of her actions, lifestyle, and speech, I have never encountered anyone who bears a greater resemblance to the Messenger of God ﷺ than Fāṭimah ؑ."[23]

> "In the Messenger of God's ﷺ speech, there was no one we observed to be more akin than Fāṭimah ؑ."[24]

> "Fāṭimah's ؑ gait mirrored that of the Prophet ﷺ."[25]

---

[22] al-Tirmidhī, Muḥammad, *Sunan al-Tirmidhī,* Vol. 5, p. 361.

[23] Ibn ʿAbd Rabbih, *al-ʿIqd al-Farīd,* Vol. 3, p. 186.

al-Ḥanafī, Muḥammad b. Yūsuf al-Zarandī, *Naẓm Durar al-Simṭayn,* p. 180.

[24] Ṭūsī, Shaykh Muḥammad b. Ḥasan, *al-Amālī,* p. 400.

al-Nisāʾī, Aḥmad b. Shuʿayb, *Sunan al-Kubra,* Vol. 7, p. 101.

[25] Ṣadūq, Shaykh Muḥammad b. ʿAlī, *al-Amālī,* p. 595.

Ibn Ḥanbal, Aḥmad, *Musnad Aḥmad b. Ḥanbal,* Vol. 6, p. 282.

"And, except her father, I witnessed no one more truthful than Fāṭimah ﷺ."[26]

[26] Ibn Shahrāshūb, Muḥammad b. ʿAlī, *Manāqib Āl Abī Ṭālib,* Vol. 3, p. 341.

Mawṣilī, Abī Yaʿla, *Musnad Abī Yaʿla,* Vol. 8, p. 153.

Reflection of the Ahl al-Bayt ﷺ

In the Noble Qur'ān, God ﷻ reveals the mystery behind the magnificence of the Ahl al-Bayt ﷺ — their purity. They are chosen beings who have shielded their souls from impurity and sin and can receive God's most profound knowledge, truth, and secrets ﷻ. Consequently, divine wisdom emanates like a flowing stream of Kawthar from their theoretical and practical way of life. This pure lineage is a single light, and there is no difference in their ranks, irrespective of gender.

Any theoretical or practical perfection proves Ahl al-Bayt's integrity and purity ﷺ. Like their counterpart, the Noble Qur'ān, purity in thought and action is also fixed for Sayyidah Fāṭimah ﷺ, and she will also be included as that source of reference. Like her precious counterpart, Imām 'Alī ﷺ explained divine teachings and interpreted the Noble Qur'ān and benefits from the source of divine grace with other members of the enlightened household ﷺ, and the difference between them is only related to their responsibilities and duties.

Sayyidah Fāṭimah ﷺ gleams as brilliantly as her equal, 'Alī al-Murtaḍā ﷺ, reflecting the entirety of Ahl al-Bayt so profoundly that even her flawless descendants adhere to her lifestyle. This is exemplified in the letters of Imām Muḥammad al-Mahdī ﷺ, where he states:

> "And in the daughter of the Messenger of God ﷺ, there is a beautiful example for me."[27]

Therefore, gaining insight and comprehension of her is essential for anyone searching for enlightenment.[28]

---

[27] Ṭabrisī, Shaykh Aḥmad b. 'Alī Ṭabrisī, *al-Iḥtijāj*, Vol. 2, p. 467.

Majlisī, 'Allamah Muḥammad Bāqir, *Biḥār al-Anwār*, Vol. 53, p. 180.

[28] Āmulī, Āyatullāh 'Abd Allāh Jawādī, *Sarchishmah Andīshah*, Vol. 2, p. 65.

An Exemplar for Both Genders

When we think of Sayyidah Fāṭimah 🕊 as a role model, we often associate her with being an ideal figure for believing women, such as daughters, wives, and mothers. We might even think that her influence is limited to women due to gender. However, this perception is not accurate. Sayyidah Fāṭimah 🕊 transcends gender boundaries as a role model. The presence of a flawless human being, irrespective of their gender, serves as a beacon of guidance, development, and evolution for all of humanity. Their speech, conduct, and thought, which stem from their impeccable and infallible soul, can benefit every individual. This is why the Prophet 🕊 and the infallible Imāms 🕊, who are male, are presented as role models for all of humanity, encompassing both men and women.[29] This indicates that they serve as role models for all genders. From the viewpoint of the Noble Qurʾān, a person who attains piety becomes a guiding light for others. If the individual is male, he inspires not just men but all people. Likewise, if the individual is female, her influence extends to all people, not just women.

Hence, from the perspective of the Noble Qurʾān, a virtuous woman is not merely a model for other women but an exemplary figure. Similarly, a virtuous man is not just a model for other men but an exemplary figure. Therefore, anyone who is virtuous, irrespective of their

---

[29] Āmulī, Āyatullāh ʿAbd Allāh Jawādī, *Zan dar Āynah Jalāl wa Jamāl*, p. 152.

gender, serves as a beacon for all of humanity.[30] The Noble Qur'ān explicitly affirms this, and when it presents individuals as role models, it cites four women as exemplary figures – two positive and two negative examples. It illustrates the example of wrongdoers by narrating the stories of two misguided women:

﴿ضَرَبَ اللَّهُ مَثَلًا لِلَّذِينَ كَفَرُوا امرَأَتَ نوحٍ وَامرَأَتَ لوطٍ﴾

﴿daraba llāhu mathalan li-lladhīna kafarū mra'ata nūḥin wa-mra'ata lūṭin﴾

﴿God draws an example for the faithless: the wife of Nūḥ and the wife of Lūṭ (Lot)﴾[31]

God ﷻ has clearly illustrated the wives of Prophet Nūḥ and Lūṭ عليهما السلام as examples for those who disbelieve. He did not present them as bad women but as representations of unbelieving and mischievous people. Similarly, He introduced virtuous women as role models for the righteous[32]:

﴿وَضَرَبَ اللَّهُ مَثَلًا لِلَّذِينَ آمَنُوا امرَأَتَ فِرعَونَ﴾

30 Ibid., p. 154.

31 Sūrat at-Taḥrīm, Verse 10.

32 Āmulī, Āyatullāh 'Abd Allāh Jawādī, *Zan dar Āynah Jalāl wa Jamāl*, p. 153-155.

﴾wa-ḍaraba llāhu mathalan li-lladhīna ʾāmanū mraʾata firʿawna﴿

﴾God draws an[other] example for those who have faith: the wife of Pharaoh﴿[33]

The heart of this matter lies in the Qurʾānic view that the essence of every human being is their soul, and the physical body is merely an instrument for this soul throughout life. This soul is genderless; therefore, attributing a person's perfection to a specific gender is flawed.[34] Moreover, none of the perfections of existence are dependent on being male, nor does being female hinder one from achieving perfection. From this perspective, true perfection, which is to attain the pinnacle of divine will, is bestowed upon every purified individual who fulfills the following prerequisites:

﴿مَن عَمِلَ صالِحًا مِن ذَكَرٍ أَو أُنثىٰ وَهُوَ مُؤمِنٌ فَلَنُحيِيَنَّهُ حَياةً طَيِّبَةً ۖ وَلَنَجزِيَنَّهُم أَجرَهُم بِأَحسَنِ ما كانوا يَعمَلونَ﴾

﴾man ʿamila ṣāliḥan min dhakarin ʾaw ʾunthā wa-huwa muʾminun fa-la-nuḥyiyannahū ḥayātan ṭayyibatan wa-la-najziyannahum ʾajrahum bi-ʾaḥsani mā kānū yaʿmalūna[a]*﴿*

[33] Sūrat at-Taḥrīm, Verse 11.

[34] Ibid., p. 76-77.

﴾Whoever acts righteously, [whether] male or female, should he be faithful, —We shall revive him with a good life and pay them their reward by the best of what they used to do﴿[35]

Sayyidah Fāṭimah ﷺ radiates in the realm of excellence and virtues, just as the other infallible Imāms ﷺ do. As a flawless and infallible individual, all her words, deeds, and silences are evidence of the direct path to guidance and prosperity. As a model for achieving success, her conduct and actions serve as a guide for both men and women. Only certain roles, such as motherhood, are specific to women. These instances make up a minor part of the examples she sets. Despite these actions forming a significant part of her life, character, and speech, they stem from the ideal of reforming and developing human character as imparted by her father. This perfect trait serves as a model for transcending gender boundaries.

[35] Sūrat an-Naḥl, Verse 97.

A Timeless Role Model

A significant hurdle for young individuals in adhering to the traditions and ways of the Ahl al-Bayt عليهم السلام, particularly Sayyidah Fāṭimah عليها السلام, is the disparity between the conditions of their time and the present. It is evident that various factors such as social circumstances, family, culture, society, ethnicity, race, and customs significantly influence an individual's life and shape their behaviors and models. Moreover, today's advanced communication and technology are incomparable to those of early Islām. These differences and varying requirements often deter young people from accepting the Ahl al-Bayt عليهم السلام as role models in their lives today. However, upon considering certain principles, it becomes apparent that the infallible Ahl al-Bayt عليهم السلام, including Sayyidah Fāṭimah عليها السلام, embodies a reality that transcends the confines of time and location.

First principle: In the eyes of an impartial observer, one can perceive a divine religion as a blueprint for guiding humanity towards everlasting joy and perfection, which aligns with the needs of people across all times, places, cultures, ethnicities, and other variable factors. The guidance is tailored to individuals' dignity, capacity, and needs. As such, the infallible leaders can be recognized as perfect human beings and fitting models for everyone. Based on their traditions and lifestyles, one can depend on them to attain happiness. We have faith in their actions and behavior, which are tied to and transcend a specific time, place, or culture.

It is important to note that all human needs and matters can be classified into constant and variable. The unwavering dignity of a person stems from their monotheistic nature, and this dignity remains unaffected by changing circumstances. For instance, in ethics, virtues such as goodness, justice, and the avoidance of cruelty are not swayed by situational factors. The religious guidance and conduct of the Ahl al-Bayt ﷺ are founded on these unchallengeable truths. These truths are absolute and retain their significance throughout history. The permissible and forbidden actions, religious directives, and ethical suggestions conveyed to humanity through the teachings and actions of the Ahl al-Bayt ﷺ are the same and remain consistent. Hence, emulating the actions and words of Sayyidah Fāṭimah ﷺ serves as evidence of this aspect of tradition and life that is timeless and can be referred to by all of humanity. However, this does not apply to one's status, circumstances, and changing needs, such as societal customs and behaviors, clothing styles, or food preferences. The Ahl al-Bayt ﷺ also encouraged people to adhere to the customs and rules of their locality. While pursuing their divine mission, they have outlined general etiquette, traditions, and necessary limits for such instances in the realm of ethics. For instance, the principle of respecting one's neighbor is expressed in a general manner. However, the method of showing respect is left to the individual's judgment, considering their era's and location's customs.[36]

---

[36] al-Ṣadr, Shahīd Sayyid Muḥammad Bāqir al-Ṣadr, *Tafsīr al-Mawḍūʿī*, Vol. 17, p. 197.

Second principle: Due to their unique status, the infallible Ahl al-Bayt ﷺ were linked to God's ﷻ repository of divine wisdom. This knowledge was not restricted to a particular time or place. Whenever they wished, with God's ﷻ permission, they could comprehend the entirety of humanity from its beginning to its conclusion. In doing so, they occasionally revealed future events from the unseen when required. In certain instances, they would make a statement or suggest an essential action for all future generations. This implies that these sacred figures conveyed such information, taking into account the needs of all humanity throughout time. Such consideration was realized through the final Prophet of Islām ﷺ and his global mission.[37]

---

[37] Ibid.

Virtues of the Ahl al-Bayt ﷤

Moderation in Praising

A believer consistently adheres to the path of truth within the bounds of moderation. He neither oversteps what is nor neglects his responsibilities. Excessiveness deficiency and understatement are two misguided approaches typically associated with the uninformed. When articulating the virtues of the Ahl al-Bayt ﷤, not only is deficiency frowned upon, but exaggeration has no outcome other than:

> "An ignorant person can only be found at one extreme or the other."[38]

It is crucial to proceed with caution to prevent the Islāmic community from experiencing the same fate that befell Amīr al-Mu'minīn (Imām 'Alī) ؑ. He ؑ was appalled by the conduct of these two groups. He prohibited his followers from engaging in such behavior:

> "Two types of individuals will meet their downfall because of me: those who excessively adore me, and those who harbor intense hatred towards me."[39]

In his interpretation of Nahj al-Balāghah, Ibn Abī Ḥadīd ؒ recounts that the Prophet ﷺ told Amīr al-Mu'minīn ؑ:

---

[38] Sharīf Raḍī, Muḥammad b. al-Ḥusayn, *Nahj al-Balāghah*, Saying 70.

[39] Ibid., Saying 117.

> "Your situation is similar to that of ʿĪsā b. Maryam ﷺ. On one side, the Jews harbored animosity towards him, insulted him, and disrespected his mother. On the other hand, the Christians showed him affection and exalted him beyond his rightful status, [attributing to him the position of God ﷻ or God's son]."[40]

Regrettably, it appears that some individuals, under the guise of praising the Ahl al-Bayt ﷺ, falsely associate them with God ﷻ. These people recite poetry in public forums to evoke emotions and induce tears from the audience. They believe that their actions serve the infallible Ahl al-Bayt ﷺ. However, they should realize that these actions provide adversaries and prejudiced listeners with a pretext, thus becoming a cause for defamation and criticism. Such behavior fails to serve the Ahl al-Bayt ﷺ and insults them.

Furthermore, if someone knowingly and intentionally speaks such words, they will lead to apostasy, which is subject to very stringent rules and is not tolerated. Lastly, these actions contradict the teachings and ethics of the Ahl al-Bayt ﷺ.

Imām Jaʿfar al-Ṣādiq ﷺ advises his companion,

> "Oh Ismāʿīl! Avoid creating something so grand that it risks destruction. Feel free to speak about us, but

---

[40] Ibn Abī al-Ḥadīd, *Sharḥ Nahj al-Balāghah,* Vol. 8, p. 119.

remember not to overstep the limit of us being a creation."⁴¹

In other words, the initial oath he mentions underlines that we are God's selected servants and do not possess independence in avoiding harm. He then proceeds to condemn those who overstate his status, saying:

"Through their actions, they are not only assaulting God 🕮, but also the Prophet, Amīr al-Mu'minīn, Sayyidah Fāṭimah, Imām al-Ḥasan, Imām al-Ḥusayn, Imām Sajjād (Imām Zayn al-ʿĀbidīn), and Imām Muḥammad al-Bāqir 🕮..."⁴²

Imām ʿAlī 🕮 to warn others against exaggeration and also as a token of humility before the Prophet 🕮 says in one of his sermons:

"By God 🕮, if I wish, I can tell every one of you from where he has come, where he has to go and all his

---

⁴¹ Ṣaffār, Muḥammad b. Ḥassan, *Baṣāʾir al-Darajāt*, Vol. 1, p. 236.

  Majlisī, ʿAllamah Muḥammad Bāqir, *Biḥār al-Anwār*, Vol. 25, p. 279.

⁴² Majlisī, ʿAllamah Muḥammad Bāqir, *Biḥār al-Anwār*, Vol. 25, p. 279.

> affairs, but I fear lest you abandon the Messenger of God ﷺ in my favor."[43]

The Prophet often resisted expressing all the merits of Imām 'Alī ﷺ. He would frequently state,

> "By God ﷻ, if I did not fear that sections of my community would echo the sentiments that Christians expressed about Prophet 'Īsā b. Maryam ﷺ, I would have voiced certain things. Upon hearing these things, people seek blessings from the dust beneath your feet."[44]

Conversely, another faction has diminished the esteemed status of the Imāms to the point of regarding them merely as virtuous scholars. This group has inadvertently succumbed to understatement in their deliberate attempt to avoid exaggeration. Their cautious approach has led them to label nearly every narration highlighting the virtues of the Ahl al-Bayt ﷺ as excessive and beyond understanding, branding the narrators as prone to exaggeration.[45]

---

[43] Sharīf Raḍī, Muḥammad b. al-Ḥusayn, *Nahj al-Balāghah,* Sermon 175.

[44] Ibn Abī al-Ḥadīd, *Sharḥ Nahj al-Balāghah,* Vol. 18, p. 282.

Mufīd, Shaykh Muḥammad, *Kitāb al-Irshād,* Vol. 1, p. 165.

[45] Āmulī, Āyatullāh 'Abd Allāh Jawādī, *Adab Finā' al-Muqaribān,* Vol. 6, p. 308.

Answer to some doubts[46]

It is fitting to scrutinize certain instances suspected of exaggeration to demonstrate that the allegations of exaggeration in these cases are unfounded. Such claims might arise from human error or extreme measures in the campaign against exaggeration, although other motives could also be at play.

a. Extensive knowledge, infallibility, and other perfections

Those who oppose exaggeration often mistakenly view the belief in the personal perfections of the Imāms عليهم السلام and Sayyidah Fāṭimah عليها السلام, such as extensive knowledge and infallibility, as overstatements. However, this perspective is fundamentally flawed. When the infallible Imāms عليهم السلام are referred to as virtuous scholars in narrations, it is important to understand that this is merely a subset of their attributes, not the sum of their virtues. The presence of such narrations that depict Ahl al-Bayt عليهم السلام in this manner does not imply that we should diminish their status to the level of other scholars or slightly above. These titles should be attributed to them in a manner that even those who oppose exaggeration can accept so that the authority of the Ahl al-Bayt عليهم السلام is preserved in Islāmic teachings. Following the Prophet, these infallible entities are the authentic interpreters of the Noble Qur'ān and the sole expositors of the traditions. Their authority should be recognized as a

[46] Ibid., p. 316-332.

duty by others. Essentially, they serve as God's ﷻ evidence of His creation. Their followers can assert their rights in the divine court of justice by quoting their words and responding to the questions on the Day of Judgement.

Such proof is contingent upon certain conditions, primarily comprehensive and absolute knowledge. This implies knowledge that should be so profound that, first, it can provide an answer to every question posed, and second, the responses are inherently truthful. This extensive and infallible knowledge can only be attained through a special gift from God ﷻ, which we refer to as *ladanī* knowledge.[47] Indeed, typical knowledge acquired in various fields, whether religious matters, rulings, divine teachings, experimental, social, economic, or political sciences, cannot possess these two characteristics. The diversity of expert

---

[47] Ibid., p. 316.

Imām ʿAlī al-Riḍā's ؑ explanation of the term Imām:

> "The Imām is distinguished with complete excellence without seeking it or acquiring it; rather, it is a unique distinction bestowed by the bountiful Giver... Verily, the prophets and the Imāms are granted success by God, and He bestows upon them from His hidden knowledge and wisdom what He does not bestow upon others. Therefore, their knowledge surpasses the knowledge of the people of their time."

Ṣadūq, Shaykh Muḥammad b. ʿAlī, *Maʿānī al-Akhbār,* p. 98-100.

Majlisī, ʿAllamah Muḥammad Bāqir, *Biḥār al-Anwār,* Vol. 25, p. 124-127.

opinions in each of these areas is evident. If jurisprudential and expert theories are derived from accurate premises, they are deemed "excusable" regarding one's actions and responsibilities. In other words, an action justified by jurisprudential knowledge is considered valid, and the individual responsible for such an act cannot be faulted if it proves incorrect.

Conversely, mere knowledge is not enough. Eliminating any chance of error is crucial to ensure the answer is neither false nor incorrect, enabling absolute obedience. This level of certainty can only be achieved with an infallible Imām. The virtue of justice eliminates the possibility of deceit, and the potential for mistakes is eradicated solely through infallibility. In essence, only an infallible person deserves total obedience and unconditional acceptance.

This status is like the ladanī knowledge, which can only be acquired with God's ﷻ permission. Thus, the infallible Imām is not simply a virtuous scholar; his knowledge is unparalleled to any other worldly knowledge. His virtue is not comparable or equivalent to other scholars; he is a unique figure of his era.[48] Certainly, the excellence of these perfect entities ﷺ is intrinsic. However, this does not imply that they attain these imperfections effortlessly, without suffering or struggle. They, too, encounter challenges to uphold their esteemed status, exceeding the usual efforts of ordinary people. Furthermore, their efforts surpass those of others to attain these acquired perfections.[49]

b. Experiencing divine revelations and hearing angels

At times, those who claim to oppose exaggeration believe that hearing angelic voices is a form of revelation exclusive to the Prophets ﷺ. Hence, when they hear that Sayyidah Fāṭimah ﷺ or other infallible Imāms ﷺ heard the voices of angels or that something was revealed to these holy personalities ﷺ, they consider it false and categorize it as exaggerated narrations. However, this is inaccurate, as the

---

[48] Ibid., p. 319.

Imām 'Alī al-Riḍā ﷺ says:

> "The Imām is unique in his time; no one can match him, no scholar can equal him, and there is no substitute for him, no one like him, and no one comparable to him."
>
> Ṣadūq, Shaykh Muḥammad b. 'Alī, *Ma'ānī al-Akhbār,* p. 98.
>
> Majlisī, 'Allamah Muḥammad Bāqir, *Biḥār al-Anwār,* Vol. 25, p. 124.

[49] Ibid., Vol. 6, p. 319.

Noble Qur'ān has attributed hearing angelic voices and receiving revelations to individuals other than the Prophets ﷺ. It is important to note that this type of revelation does not imply a new or legislative message. After Amīr al-Mu'minīn ﷺ performed the final ghusl for the Prophet ﷺ, he stated that all such communications ceased.[50] Rather, this revelation is affirmatory.[51] Consequently, no one has asserted that the Imāms ﷺ introduced a new law through hearing angelic voices or receiving revelations, just as no one has claimed prophethood for the mother of Prophet 'Īsā ﷺ. However, the Noble Qur'ān has informed us about such interactions with the angels:

﴿فَاتَّخَذَتْ مِن دُونِهِمْ حِجَابًا فَأَرْسَلْنَا إِلَيْهَا رُوحَنَا فَتَمَثَّلَ لَهَا بَشَرًا سَوِيًّا﴾

﴿*fa-ttakhadhat min dūnihim ḥijāban fa-'arsalnā 'ilayhā rūḥanā fa-tamaththala lahā basharan sawiyya*ⁿ﴾

﴿قَالَتْ إِنِّي أَعُوذُ بِالرَّحْمَٰنِ مِنكَ إِن كُنتَ تَقِيًّا﴾

﴿*qālat 'innī 'a'ūdhu bi-r-raḥmāni minka 'in kunta taqiyya*ⁿ﴾

---

50 Sharīf Raḍī, Muḥammad b. al-Ḥusayn, *Nahj al-Balāghah*, Sermon 235.

51 Āmulī, Āyatullāh 'Abd Allāh Jawādī, *Adab Finā' al-Muqaribān*, Vol. 6, p. 319.

Āmulī, Āyatullāh 'Abd Allāh Jawādī, *Tasnīm fī Tafsīr al-Qur'ān*, Vol. 6, p. 415.

﴿قالَ إِنَّما أَنا رَسولُ رَبِّكِ لِأَهَبَ لَكِ غُلامًا زَكِيًّا﴾

﴾qāla 'innamā 'ana rasūlu rabbiki li-'ahaba laki ghulāman zakiyyaⁿ﴿

﴿قالَت أَنّىٰ يَكونُ لي غُلامٌ وَلَم يَمسَسني بَشَرٌ وَلَم أَكُ بَغِيًّا﴾

﴾qālat 'annā yakūnu lī ghulāmun wa-lam yamsasnī basharun wa-lam 'aku baghiyyaⁿ﴿

﴿قالَ كَذٰلِكِ قالَ رَبُّكِ هُوَ عَلَيَّ هَيِّنٌ ۖ وَلِنَجعَلَهُ آيَةً لِلنّاسِ وَرَحمَةً مِنّا ۚ وَكانَ أَمرًا مَقضِيًّا﴾

﴾qāla ka-dhāliki qāla rabbuki huwa 'alayya hayyinun wa-li-naj'alahū 'āyatan li-n-nāsi wa-raḥmatan minnā wa-kāna 'amran maqḍiyyaⁿ﴿

﴾Thus did she seclude herself from them, whereupon We sent to her Our Spirit and he became incarnate for her as a well-proportioned human. She said, 'I seek the protection of the All-beneficent from you, should you be Godwary!' He said, 'I am only a messenger of your Lord that I may give you a pure son.' She said, 'How shall I have a child seeing that no human being has ever touched me, nor have I been unchaste?' He said, 'So shall it be. Your Lord says, "It is simple for Me."*

And so that We may make him a sign for mankind and a mercy from Us, and it is a matter [already] decided.'[52]

So Maryam ۞ also saw an angel in human form, heard his speech, and spoke to him.

A similar occurrence can also be seen with the wife of Prophet Ibrāhīm ۞:

﴿وَلَقَدْ جَاءَتْ رُسُلُنَا إِبْرَاهِيمَ بِالْبُشْرَىٰ قَالُوا سَلَامًا قَالَ سَلَامٌ فَمَا لَبِثَ أَن جَاءَ بِعِجْلٍ حَنِيذٍ﴾

{wa-la-qad jā'at rusulunā 'ibrāhīma bi-l-bushrā qālū salāman qāla salāmun fa-mā labitha 'an jā'a bi-'ijlin ḥanīdhⁱⁿ}

﴿فَلَمَّا رَأَىٰ أَيْدِيَهُمْ لَا تَصِلُ إِلَيْهِ نَكِرَهُمْ وَأَوْجَسَ مِنْهُمْ خِيفَةً قَالُوا لَا تَخَفْ إِنَّا أُرْسِلْنَا إِلَىٰ قَوْمِ لُوطٍ﴾

{fa-lammā ra'ā 'aydiyahum lā taṣilu 'ilayhi nakirahum wa-'awjasa minhum khīfatan qālū lā takhaf 'innā 'ursilnā 'ilā qawmi lūṭⁱⁿ}

---

[52] Sūrat Maryam, Verses 17-21.

* That is, Jibrā'īl (Gabriel) ۞.

﴿وَامرَأَتُهُ قائِمَةٌ فَضَحِكَت فَبَشَّرناها بِإِسحاقَ وَمِن وَراءِ إِسحاقَ يَعقوبَ﴾

﴿*wa-mra'atuhū qā'imatun fa-ḍaḥikat fa-bashsharnāhā bi-'isḥāqa wa-min warā'i 'isḥāqa ya'qūb*[a]﴾

﴿قالَت يا وَيلَتىٰ أَأَلِدُ وَأَنا عَجوزٌ وَهٰذا بَعلي شَيخًا ۖ إِنَّ هٰذا لَشَيءٌ عَجيبٌ﴾

﴿*qālat yā-waylatā 'a-'alidu wa-'ana 'ajūzun wa-hādhā ba'lī shaykhan 'inna hādhā la-shay'un 'ajīb*[un]﴾

﴿قالوا أَتَعجَبينَ مِن أَمرِ اللَّهِ ۖ رَحمَتُ اللَّهِ وَبَرَكاتُهُ عَلَيكُم أَهلَ البَيتِ ۚ
إِنَّهُ حَميدٌ مَجيدٌ﴾

﴿*qālū 'a-ta'jabīna min 'amri llāhi raḥmatu llāhi wa-barakātuhū 'alaykum 'ahla l-bayti 'innahū ḥamīdun majīd*[un]﴾

﴿*Certainly Our messengers came to Ibrāhīm with the good news, and said, 'Peace!' 'Peace!' He replied. Presently he brought [for them] a roasted calf. But when he saw their hands not reaching for it, he took them amiss and felt a fear of them. They said, 'Do not be afraid. We have been sent to the people of Lūṭ.' His wife, standing by, laughed as We gave her the good news of [the birth of] Isḥāq (Isaac), and of Ya'qūb (Jacob), after Isḥāq. She said, 'Oh, my! Shall I, an old woman, bear [children], and [while] this husband of mine is an old man?! That is indeed an odd thing!'They said, 'Are you amazed at God's dispensation? [That is] God's mercy and His blessings upon you, members of the household. Indeed He is Laudable, Glorious.*﴿[53]

The mother of Prophet Mūsā ؑ was not a prophet herself. However, she received divine guidance instructing her to place her infant in a basket and set it afloat down the river:

﴿وَأَوحَينا إِلىٰ أُمِّ موسىٰ أَن أَرضِعيهِ ۖ فَإِذا خِفتِ عَلَيهِ فَأَلقيهِ فِي اليَمِّ وَلا تَخافي وَلا تَحزَني ۖ إِنّا رادّوهُ إِلَيكِ وَجاعِلوهُ مِنَ المُرسَلينَ﴾

﴾*wa-'awḥaynā 'ilā 'ummi mūsā 'an 'arḍi'īhi fa-'idhā khifti 'alayhi fa-'alqīhi fī l-yammi wa-lā takhāfī wa-lā taḥzanī 'innā rāddūhu 'ilayki wa-jā'ilūhu mina l-mursalīn*[a]﴿

﴾*We revealed to Mūsā's mother, [saying], 'Nurse him; then, when you fear for him, cast him into the river, and do not fear or grieve, for We will restore him to you and make him one of the apostles.*'﴿[54]

These kinds of revelations are not linked to prophethood. In response, it is important to clarify that no one has suggested that the infallible Imāms ؑ receive legislative revelations or that angels descended upon them to deliver a new sharī'ah. Instead, the term 'revelation' in this context is used to denote an indication and affirmation of the previous message (of the Prophet ﷺ). These can be

---

[53] Sūrat Hūd, Verses 69-73.

[54] Sūrat al-Qaṣaṣ, Verse 7.

interpreted as inspirations and occasionally as explanations of certain teachings of Prophet Muḥammad ﷺ.[55]

Having established that receiving revelations and witnessing angels are not exclusively tied to prophethood and that it is possible for other chosen individuals, it is enough to consider the Qur'ānic argument in Sūrat al-Qadr.[56]

﴿تَنَزَّلُ الْمَلَائِكَةُ وَالرُّوحُ فِيهَا بِإِذْنِ رَبِّهِم مِّن كُلِّ أَمْرٍ﴾

﴾*tanazzalu l-malā'ikatu wa-r-rūḥu fīhā bi-'idhni rabbihim min kulli 'amrin*﴿

﴾*In it the angels and the Spirit descend, by the leave of their Lord, with every command*﴿[57]

This verse states that all the angels descending on this night reveal the secrets of the coming year. The question arises: who are these secrets revealed to, and who receives them? Could anyone other than an infallible Imām accommodate

---

[55] Āmulī, Āyatullāh 'Abd Allāh Jawādī, *Adab Fināʾ al-Muqaribān,* Vol. 6, p. 138-139.

[56] This argument is a Qur'ānic argument not based on narrations, so no one can consider its argument excessive or far-fetched. However, it is important to note that both Qur'ānic and narrative arguments serve as evidence for us.

[57] Sūrat al-Qadr, Verse 4.

these angels and their many teachings and important news?[58]

c. Knowing the condition of the Shīʿah community

It is sometimes claimed that this belief that the Imām knew about the condition of every Shīʿah is an incorrect belief based on exaggeration. The reason for such a claim is that the knowledge of such holy persons after their death is meaningless because a dead person has no consciousness – regardless of whether he is an Imām or not. Even during his lifetime, the Imām ﷺ only sees his surroundings, and knowledge of the hidden actions of the Shīʿah requires a knowledge of the unseen. Those who claim that they knew the unseen are exaggerating, just as the claim of a visitor hearing the voice of one of these holy personalities is baseless. The answer to such an argument is as follows:

Many verses indicate that the Prophet is a witness to his nation's actions:

﴿وَيَكُونَ الرَّسُولُ عَلَيكُم شَهِيدًا﴾

﴾*wa-yakūna r-rasūlu ʿalaykum shahīdan*﴿

﴾*and that the Apostle may be a witness to you*﴿[59]

---

[58] Āmulī, Āyatullāh ʿAbd Allāh Jawādī, *Adab Finā' al-Muqaribān*, Vol. 1, p. 142-143.

[59] Sūrat al-Baqarah, Verse 143.

﴿لِيَكُونَ الرَّسولُ شَهيدًا عَلَيكُم﴾

﴿li-yakūna r-rasūlu shahīdan ʿalaykum﴾

﴿so that the Apostle may be a witness to you﴾[60]

Moreover, similarly, he was also a witness to the actions of previous nations:

﴿فَكَيفَ إِذا جِئنا مِن كُلِّ أُمَّةٍ بِشَهيدٍ وَجِئنا بِكَ عَلىٰ هٰؤُلاءِ شَهيدًا﴾

﴿fa-kayfa ʾidhā jiʾnā min kulli ʾummatin bi-shahīdin wa-jiʾnā bika ʿalā hāʾulāʾi shahīdaⁿ﴾

﴿So how shall it be, when We bring from every nation a witness and We bring you *as a witness to them?﴾*[61]

﴿وَيَومَ نَبعَثُ في كُلِّ أُمَّةٍ شَهيدًا عَلَيهِم مِن أَنفُسِهِم ۖ
وَجِئنا بِكَ شَهيدًا عَلىٰ هٰؤُلاءِ﴾

﴿wa-yawma nabʿathu fī kulli ʾummatin shahīdan ʿalayhim min ʾanfusihim wa-jiʾnā bika shahīdan ʿalā hāʾulāʾi﴾

---

[60] Sūrat al-Ḥajj, Verse 78.

[61] Sūrat an-Nisāʾ, Verse 41.

﴾*The day We raise in every nation a witness against them from among themselves, We shall bring* you *as a witness against these*﴿[62]

Similarly, Prophet ʿĪsā ﷺ witnessed his nation's actions:

﴾وَيَومَ القِيامَةِ يَكونُ عَلَيهِم شَهيدًا﴿

﴾*wa-yawma l-qiyāmati yakūnu ʿalayhim shahīdaⁿ*﴿

﴾*and on the Day of Resurrection he will be a witness against them**﴿[63]

The Day of Judgment serves as a platform for bearing witness. However, before one can testify, one must be definitive about what one is testifying. Therefore, before the Prophet ﷺ can testify about the deeds of his people, he must have witnessed or known these actions before Judgment Day. The question arises when we consider that centuries have passed since the Holy Prophet's ﷺ demise or Prophet ʿĪsā's ﷺ ascension. If their death or absence prevents them from witnessing their people's actions, how can they personally testify before God ﷻ on Judgment Day

[62] Sūrat an-Naḥl, Verse 89.

[63] Sūrat an-Nisāʾ, Verse 159.

* That is, every Jew or Christian, before dying, will believe in the Prophet Muḥammad ﷺ, or, according to another interpretation, in ʿĪsā (Jesus) ﷺ.

about their people's deeds? Furthermore, in such an understanding, testifying about the people of their era is also challenging, as they were not always physically present with each individual.

In addition, a group of believers are also mentioned as witnesses for the actions of the Islāmic nation:

﴿لِتَكونوا شُهَداءَ عَلَى النّاسِ﴾

﴿*li-takūnū shuhadā'a 'alā n-nāsi*﴾

﴿*that you may be witnesses to the people*﴾[64]

﴿وَتَكونوا شُهَداءَ عَلَى النّاسِ﴾

﴿*wa-takūnū shuhadā'a 'alā n-nāsi*﴾

﴿*and that you may be witnesses to mankind*﴾[65]

﴿وَقُلِ اعمَلوا فَسَيَرَى اللَّهُ عَمَلَكُم وَرَسولُهُ وَالمُؤمِنونَ﴾

﴿*wa-quli 'malū fa-sa-yarā llāhu 'amalakum wa-rasūluhū wa-l-mu'minūna*﴾

---

[64] Sūrat al-Baqarah, Verse 143.

[65] Sūrat al-Ḥajj, Verse 78.

﴾And say, 'Go on working: God will see your conduct, and His Apostle and the faithful [as well]﴿[66]

If these faithful individuals, regardless of their identity, are deceased (and presumed incapable of acquiring this knowledge), observing the deeds of other believers, as with the Prophet ﷺ, would pose a challenge. This issue would also arise during their lifetimes, as they could not observe all believers' actions without knowing the unseen.

The conclusion is that the Holy Prophet ﷺ and other prophets ﷺ have knowledge of the unseen and are aware of the condition of their nation even after their death. They hear the words of the believers when they perform visitation or prayers – wherever they may be – when they send their salutations to the Prophet ﷺ, saying, "Peace be upon the Prophet ﷺ, and may God's Mercy and Blessings be upon you." Thus, the ability to hear the believer's voice is not confined to those currently present at the shrines. Believers can send their greetings from any location worldwide, and the prophets will hear them. Therefore, it is incorrect to accept a viewpoint that contradicts this as it contradicts the Noble Qur'ān.

Moreover, certain exceptional believers are known to observe actions and hear their voices, possessing knowledge of the unseen, with numerous historical instances

---

[66] Sūrat at-Tawbah, Verse 105.

supporting this. Is it possible to suggest that the people of a nation possess this ability, but their Imām does not?

Based on certain verses of the Noble Qur'ān, it could be argued that the knowledge of the unseen is exclusively held by God ﷻ. However, other verses imply that some divine prophets ﷺ benefitted from this knowledge. When considering all these verses, several insights can be gathered. The topic of unseen knowledge and the reconciliation of these seemingly contradictory verses has been explored and clarified in various texts.[67] In summary, a suitable approach is to categorize unseen knowledge into two types: intrinsic and indirect. Intrinsic knowledge of the unseen includes attributes such as power, life, honor, creation, destruction, etc. This kind of knowledge is inherent to its possessor without an intermediary. On the other hand, indirect knowledge of the unseen is a form of knowledge that has been bestowed upon its holder. While intrinsic knowledge is the domain of God ﷻ alone, He ﷻ has also chosen certain believers like the Prophets ﷺ and the Ahl al-Bayt ﷺ to partake in this knowledge. For example, the following verse is about inherent knowledge of the unseen:

﴿فَقُل إِنَّمَا الغَيبُ لِلَّهِ﴾

﴾*fa-qul 'innamā l-ghaybu li-llāhi*﴿

[67] Āmulī, Āyatullāh 'Abd Allāh Jawādī, *Adab Finā' al-Muqaribān*, Vol. 3, p. 416.

﴾*Say, '[The knowledge of] the Unseen belongs only to God*﴿[68]

The following verse, which attributes Prophet ʿĪsā ﷺ with the knowledge of the unseen, is about his indirect and gifted knowledge of the unseen:

﴿وَأُنَبِّئُكُم بِمَا تَأْكُلُونَ وَمَا تَدَّخِرُونَ فِي بُيُوتِكُمْ﴾

﴾*wa-'unabbi'ukum bi-mā ta'kulūna wa-mā taddakhirūna fī buyūtikum*﴿

﴾*And I will tell you what you have eaten and what you have stored in your houses*﴿[69]

d. Performing miracles

Some view the accounts of miracles and extraordinary deeds performed by the Imāms ﷺ as instances of exaggeration. However, even those special servants of God ﷻ who had not attained the rank of imamate could perform miracles. The Noble Qur'ān bears witness to such individuals who were not prophets; for instance:

﴿كُلَّمَا دَخَلَ عَلَيْهَا زَكَرِيَّا الْمِحْرَابَ وَجَدَ عِندَهَا رِزْقًا ۖ قَالَ يَا مَرْيَمُ أَنَّىٰ لَكِ هَٰذَا ۖ قَالَتْ هُوَ مِنْ عِندِ اللَّهِ ۖ إِنَّ اللَّهَ يَرْزُقُ مَن يَشَاءُ بِغَيْرِ حِسَابٍ﴾

[68] Sūrat Yūnus, Verse 20.

[69] Sūrat Āl 'Imrān, Verse 49.

﴿kullamā dakhala 'alayhā zakariyyā l-miḥrāba wajada 'indahā rizqan qāla yā-maryamu 'annā laki hādhā qālat huwa min 'indi llāhi 'inna llāha yarzuqu man yashā'u bi-ghayri ḥisāb[in]﴾

﴿Whenever Zakariyyā visited her in the sanctuary, he would find provisions with her. He said, 'O Mary, from where does this come for you?' She said, 'It comes from God. God provides whomever He wishes without any reckoning.'﴾[70]

We also see in the instance of Āṣif b. Barkhiyā, who managed to transport the throne of Queen Ṣaba' (Sheba) to Prophet Sulaymān ﷺ in an instant:[71]

﴿قَالَ الَّذِي عِندَهُ عِلْمٌ مِّنَ الْكِتَابِ أَنَا آتِيكَ بِهِ قَبْلَ أَن يَرْتَدَّ إِلَيْكَ طَرْفُكَ ۚ فَلَمَّا رَآهُ مُسْتَقِرًّا عِندَهُ قَالَ هَٰذَا مِن فَضْلِ رَبِّي﴾

﴿qāla lladhī 'indahū 'ilmun mina l-kitābi 'ana 'ātīka bihī qabla 'an yartadda 'ilayka ṭarfuka fa-lammā ra'āhu mustaqirran 'indahū qāla hādhā min faḍli rabbī﴾

[70] Sūrat Āl 'Imrān, Verse 37.

[71] Ibn al-Maghāzlī, *Manāqīb al-Imām 'Alī b. Abī Ṭālib*, Vol. 2, p. 324.

﴾*The one who had knowledge of the Book* said, 'I will bring it to you in the twinkling of an eye.' So when he saw it set near him, he said, 'This is by the grace of my Lord...'*﴿[72]

Some might argue that the feats of Āṣif b. Barkhiyā were only achievable through Prophet Sulaymān ﷺ, not independently, or the remarkable event involving Maryam ﷺ[73] were due to Prophet 'Īsā ﷺ, not because of Maryam ﷺ's merit. However, this can be countered by stating that the deeds of Amīr al-Mu'minīn ﷺ and the other Imāms ﷺ are likewise a continuation of the miracles of the Prophet ﷺ.[74] Therefore, the honor and extraordinary accomplishments of someone other than the Prophet ﷺ cannot be dismissed in any way.

In the tafsīr (*exegesis*) of the Noble Qur'ān, there is a lengthy discussion of what is meant by the following extract in verse:

﴿وَمَنْ عِندَهُۥ عِلْمُ الْكِتَابِ﴾

﴾*wa-man 'indahū 'ilmu l-kitābⁱ*﴿

[72] Sūrat an-Naml, Verse 40.

* He is said to have been Sulaymān's vizier and successor, Āṣif b. Barkhiyā.

[73] Extraordinary events that occur as a prelude to prophethood.

[74] 'Allāmah Ḥillī, Ḥasan b. Yūsuf, *Kashf al-Murād*, p. 351.

‹and he who possesses the knowledge of the Book›[75]

Moreover, this person is not the Prophet ﷺ but must be someone else. Through using this verse as well as the following narration:

"The one who knew the Book said..."

one can say that it suggests any person[76] who knows part of the book can perform extraordinary miracles greater than that of Āṣif b. Barkhiyā:

Sudayr narrates:

"Myself and a group of others, including Abū Baṣīr, were sitting with Imām Jaʿfar al-Ṣādiq ﷦. Suddenly, he ﷦ got up angrily and left. Upon returning, he ﷦ said:

'I am stunned at those who say that we know the unseen, while only God ﷻ possesses that knowledge. I thought to discipline our housemaid,

---

[75] Sūrat ar-Raʿd, Verse 43.

[76] Based on a narration, the verse is about Amīr al-Muʾminīn ﷦ and the other Imāms ﷦.

al-ʿAyyāshī, Muḥammad b. Masʿūd, *Tafsīr al-ʿAyyāshī,*
    Vol. 2, p. 220-221.

al-Ḥuwayzī, al-ʿArūsī, *Tafsīr Nūr al-Thaqalayn,* Vol. 2, p. 522.

so and so, and could not find in which quarter she was in.'"

Sudayr says:

"When the meeting was over, and the Imām 🕮 went home, I, Abū Baṣīr, and Muyassir went to his house. We told him,

'May God 🕮 take our souls in service for your cause. We heard you say so and so about your housemaid, but we know you have much knowledge. We do not say that you possess the knowledge of the unseen.'

He 🕮 replied:

'Oh Sudayr, Do you not read the Noble Qurʾān?'

I replied positively.

He 🕮 continued:

'Upon reading, have you come across the following words of God 🕮?'

❲The one who knew the Book said, 'I will bring it to you in the twinkling of an eye'❳[77]

---

[77] Sūrat an-Naml, Verse 40.

I replied positively.

The Imām ﷺ said:

> 'Do you know who the man is? Do you know how much knowledge of the Book he had?'

I said:

> 'Please tell me about his knowledge?'

The Imām ﷺ said:

> 'His knowledge of the Book was like one drop compared to the green ocean (Atlantic).'

I replied:

> 'My Imām, that is very little.'

The Imām ﷺ replied:

> 'Oh Sudayr! This little amount would be great if God ﷻ mentioned it in His book. Have you read the verse:

﴿قُلْ كَفَىٰ بِاللَّهِ شَهِيدًا بَيْنِي وَبَيْنَكُمْ وَمَنْ عِندَهُ عِلْمُ الْكِتَابِ﴾

﴾qul kafā bi-llāhi shahīdan baynī wa-baynakum wa-man ʿindahū ʿilmu l-kitābi﴿

﴾Say, *'God suffices as a witness between me and you, and he who possesses the knowledge of the Book'*﴿[78]

I replied to him positively.

He ﷺ then said:

> 'Is the knowledge of one who possesses the knowledge of the whole book greater or that of the one who possesses some knowledge of the Book?'

Then he ﷺ took his blessed hand and pointed to his chest saying:

> 'The knowledge of the whole Book, I swear by God ﷻ, is with us.'"[79]

This account indicates that the initial instance where the Imām ﷺ refuted knowing the unseen was because there were unfamiliar individuals or those with weak faith and comprehension present. These individuals could potentially cause complications for the Imām ﷺ and his followers. However, in the subsequent assembly, this issue was no longer a concern, and the Imām ﷺ unambiguously elucidated the reality of the situation.[80]

---

[78] Sūrat ar-Ra'd, Verse 43.

[79] Kulaynī, Shaykh Muḥammad b. Ya'qūb, *al-Kāfī*, Vol. 1, p. 257.

[80] Āmulī, Āyatullāh 'Abd Allāh Jawādī, *Adab Finā' al-Muqaribān*, Vol. 6, p. 326.

e. The superiority of Imāms ﷺ over previous prophets

Those who argue against exaggeration often view the belief in the Imām's supremacy over the prophet as a case of exaggeration. This denial stems from nothing more than apparent exclusion. However, such exclusion can be dispelled with a straightforward comparison: It is not unreasonable to suggest that a teaching assistant at a top-tier university who has not yet ascended to a full teaching position could hold a higher status than a regular primary school teacher. This is because the teaching assistant's work is exemplary, and the issues they handle are likely more challenging.

Divine laws have been presented to humanity much like lessons in academic classrooms, with earlier laws serving as the initial divine classrooms in the educational system of human society. Therefore, it is not contradictory for a prophet of earlier nations to have a lower status than the one responsible for the final nation. In essence, being a prophet or attaining the status of God's close friend ﷺ does not necessarily imply superiority in all aspects. This can be observed in the lives of the prophets ﷺ, such as when Prophet Mūsā ﷺ was introduced as a student of Khiḍr ﷺ:

﴿فَوَجَدَا عَبْدًا مِنْ عِبَادِنَا آتَيْنَاهُ رَحْمَةً مِنْ عِنْدِنَا وَعَلَّمْنَاهُ مِنْ لَدُنَّا عِلْمًا﴾

﴿*fa-wajadā ʿabdan min ʿibādinā ʾātaynāhu raḥmatan min ʿindinā wa-ʿallamnāhu min ladunnā ʿilma*ⁿ﴾

﴿قَالَ لَهُ مُوسَىٰ هَلْ أَتَّبِعُكَ عَلَىٰ أَن تُعَلِّمَنِ مِمَّا عُلِّمْتَ رُشْدًا﴾

﴿*qāla lahū mūsā hal ʾattabiʿuka ʿalā ʾan tuʿallimani mimmā ʿullimta rushdan*﴾

﴿قَالَ إِنَّكَ لَن تَسْتَطِيعَ مَعِيَ صَبْرًا﴾

﴿*qāla ʾinnaka lan tastaṭīʿa maʿiya ṣabran*﴾

﴿وَكَيْفَ تَصْبِرُ عَلَىٰ مَا لَمْ تُحِطْ بِهِ خُبْرًا﴾

﴿*wa-kayfa taṣbiru ʿalā mā lam tuḥiṭ bihī khubran*﴾

﴿قَالَ سَتَجِدُنِي إِن شَاءَ اللَّهُ صَابِرًا وَلَا أَعْصِي لَكَ أَمْرًا﴾

﴿*qāla sa-tajidunī ʾin shāʾa llāhu ṣābiran wa-lā ʾaʿṣī laka ʾamran*﴾

﴿قَالَ فَإِنِ اتَّبَعْتَنِي فَلَا تَسْأَلْنِي عَن شَيْءٍ حَتَّىٰ أُحْدِثَ لَكَ مِنْهُ ذِكْرًا﴾

﴿*qāla fa-ʾini ttabaʿtanī fa-lā tasʾalnī ʿan shayʾin ḥattā ʾuḥditha laka minhu dhikran*﴾

﴿فَانطَلَقَا حَتَّىٰ إِذَا رَكِبَا فِي السَّفِينَةِ خَرَقَهَا ۖ قَالَ أَخَرَقْتَهَا لِتُغْرِقَ أَهْلَهَا لَقَدْ جِئْتَ شَيْئًا إِمْرًا﴾

﴿*fa-nṭalaqā ḥattā ʾidhā rakibā fī s-safīnati kharaqahā qāla ʾa-kharaqtahā li-tughriqa ʾahlahā la-qad jiʾta shayʾan ʾimran*﴾

﴿قَالَ أَلَمْ أَقُلْ إِنَّكَ لَن تَسْتَطِيعَ مَعِيَ صَبْرًا﴾

﴿*qāla ʾa-lam ʾaqul ʾinnaka lan tastaṭīʿa maʿiya ṣabran*﴾

﴿قَالَ لَا تُؤَاخِذْنِي بِمَا نَسِيتُ وَلَا تُرْهِقْنِي مِنْ أَمْرِي عُسْرًا﴾

﴿*qāla lā tuʾākhidhnī bi-mā nasītu wa-lā turhiqnī min ʾamrī ʿusran*﴾

﴿فَانطَلَقَا حَتَّىٰ إِذَا لَقِيَا غُلَامًا فَقَتَلَهُ قَالَ أَقَتَلْتَ نَفْسًا زَكِيَّةً بِغَيْرِ نَفْسٍ لَّقَدْ جِئْتَ شَيْئًا نُّكْرًا﴾

﴿*fa-nṭalaqā ḥattā ʾidhā laqiyā ghulāman fa-qatalahū qāla ʾa-qatalta nafsan zakiyyatan bi-ghayri nafsin la-qad jiʾta shayʾan nukran*﴾

﴿قَالَ أَلَمْ أَقُل لَّكَ إِنَّكَ لَن تَسْتَطِيعَ مَعِيَ صَبْرًا﴾

﴿*qāla ʾa-lam ʾaqul laka ʾinnaka lan tastaṭīʿa maʿiya ṣabran*﴾

﴿قَالَ إِن سَأَلْتُكَ عَن شَيْءٍ بَعْدَهَا فَلَا تُصَاحِبْنِي ۖ قَدْ بَلَغْتَ مِن لَّدُنِّي عُذْرًا﴾

﴾*qāla ʾin saʾaltuka ʿan shayʾin baʿdahā fa-lā tuṣāḥibnī qad balaghta min ladunnī ʿudhra*^{n}﴿

﴿فَانطَلَقا حَتّىٰ إِذا أَتَيا أَهلَ قَريَةٍ استَطعَما أَهلَها فَأَبَوا أَن يُضَيِّفوهُما فَوَجَدا
فيها جِدارًا يُريدُ أَن يَنقَضَّ فَأَقامَهُ ۖ قالَ لَو شِئتَ لَاتَّخَذتَ عَلَيهِ أَجرًا﴾

﴾*fa-nṭalaqā ḥattā ʾidhā ʾatayā ʾahla qaryatin-i staṭʿamā ʾahlahā fa-ʾabaw ʾan yuḍayyifūhumā fa-wajadā fīhā jidāran yurīdu ʾan yanqaḍḍa fa-ʾaqāmahū qāla law shiʾta la-ttakhadhta ʿalayhi ʾajra*^{n}﴿

﴿قالَ هٰذا فِراقُ بَيني وَبَينِكَ ۚ سَأُنَبِّئُكَ بِتَأويلِ ما لَم تَستَطِع عَلَيهِ صَبرًا﴾

﴾*qāla hādhā firāqu baynī wa-baynika sa-ʾunabbiʾuka bi-taʾwīli mā lam tastaṭiʿ ʿalayhi ṣabra*^{n}﴿

﴿أَمَّا السَّفينَةُ فَكانَت لِمَساكينَ يَعمَلونَ فِي البَحرِ فَأَرَدتُ أَن
أَعيبَها وَكانَ وَراءَهُم مَلِكٌ يَأخُذُ كُلَّ سَفينَةٍ غَصبًا﴾

﴾*ʾammā s-safīnatu fa-kānat li-masākīna yaʿmalūna fī l-baḥri fa-ʾaradtu ʾan ʾaʿībahā wa-kāna warāʾahum malikun yaʾkhudhu kulla safīnatin ghaṣba*^{n}﴿

﴿وَأَمَّا الغُلامُ فَكانَ أَبَواهُ مُؤمِنَينِ فَخَشينا أَن يُرهِقَهُما طُغيانًا وَكُفرًا﴾

﴾*wa-ʾammā l-ghulāmu fa-kānā ʾabawāhu muʾminayni fa-khashīnā ʾan yurhiqahumā ṭughyānan wa-kufra*^{n}﴿

﴿فَأَرَدنا أَن يُبدِلَهُما رَبُّهُما خَيرًا مِنهُ زَكاةً وَأَقرَبَ رُحمًا﴾

﴾fa-ʾaradnā ʾan yubdilahumā rabbuhumā khayran minhu zakātan wa-ʾaqraba ruḥman﴿

﴿وَأَمَّا الجِدارُ فَكانَ لِغُلامَينِ يَتيمَينِ فِي المَدينَةِ وَكانَ تَحتَهُ كَنزٌ لَهُما وَكانَ أَبوهُما صالِحًا فَأَرادَ رَبُّكَ أَن يَبلُغا أَشُدَّهُما وَيَستَخرِجا كَنزَهُما رَحمَةً مِن رَبِّكَ ۚ وَما فَعَلتُهُ عَن أَمري ۚ ذٰلِكَ تَأويلُ ما لَم تَسطِع عَلَيهِ صَبرًا﴾

﴾wa-ʾammā l-jidāru fa-kāna li-ghulāmayni yatīmayni fī l-madīnati wa-kāna taḥtahū kanzun lahumā wa-kāna ʾabūhumā ṣāliḥan fa-ʾarāda rabbuka ʾan yablughā ʾashuddahumā wa-yastakhrijā kanzahumā raḥmatan min rabbika wa-mā faʿaltuhū ʿan ʾamrī dhālika taʾwīlu mā lam tasṭiʿ ʿalayhi ṣabran﴿

﴾[There] they found one of Our servants whom We had granted a mercy from Ourselves, and taught him a knowledge from Our own. Mūsā said to him, 'May I follow you for the purpose that you teach me some of the probity you have been taught?' He said, 'Indeed you cannot have patience with me! And how can you have patience about something you are not in the know of?' He said, 'You will find me, God willing, to be patient, and I will not disobey you in any matter.' He said, 'If you follow me, do not question me concerning anything until I [myself] make a mention of it to you.' So they went on. When they boarded the boat, he made a hole in it. He said, 'Did you make a hole in it to drown its

people? You have certainly done a monstrous thing!' He said, 'Did I not say, indeed you cannot have patience with me?' He said, 'Do not take me to task for my forgetting, and do not be hard upon me.' So they went on. When they encountered a boy, he slew him. He said, 'Did you slay an innocent soul, without [his having slain] anyone? You have certainly done a dire thing!' He said, 'Did I not tell you, indeed you cannot have patience with me?' He said, 'If I question you about anything after this, do not keep me in your company. You have already got sufficient excuse on my part.' So they went on. When they came to the people of a town, they asked its people for food, but they refused to extend them any hospitality. There they found a wall which was about to collapse, so he erected it. He said, 'Had you wished, you could have taken a wage for it.' He said, 'This is where you and I shall part. I will inform you about the interpretation of that over which you could not maintain patience. As for the boat, it belonged to some poor people who work on the sea. I wanted to make it defective, for behind them was a king seizing every ship usurpingly. As for the boy, his parents were faithful [persons], and We feared he would overwhelm them with rebellion and unfaith. So We desired that their Lord should give them in exchange one better than him in respect of purity and closer in mercy. As for the wall, it belonged to two boy orphans in the city. Under it there was a treasure belonging to them. Their father had been a righteous man. So your Lord desired that they should come of age and take out their treasure —as a mercy from your Lord. I did not do that out of my own accord. This is the interpretation of that over which you could not maintain patience.'[81]

Therefore, from a logical standpoint, it is not unreasonable to hold such a belief, and there is no justification for dismissing this belief based solely on titles. In addition to establishing this superiority, it is not illogical to believe that Imām ʿAlī 🌸, Sayyidah Fāṭimah 🌸, and the Ahl al-Bayt 🌸 achieved a higher status and reached greater levels of perfection than earlier prophets 🌸, even though they were not tasked with delivering the message. Moreover, numerous narrations support this assertion.[82]

With the aid of some Qurʾānic verses, it becomes clear that the Ahl al-Bayt 🌸 was superior to previous prophets 🌸:

1. The Ahl al-Bayt 🌸 is introduced as purified (Purification Verse):

﴿إِنَّمَا يُرِيدُ اللَّهُ لِيُذْهِبَ عَنْكُمُ الرِّجْسَ أَهْلَ البَيْتِ وَيُطَهِّرَكُمْ تَطْهِيرًا﴾

'innamā yurīdu llāhu li-yudhhiba ʿankumu r-rijsa 'ahla l-bayti wa-yuṭahhirakum taṭhīraⁿ'

---

[81] Sūrat al-Kahf, Verse 65-82.

[82] Āmulī, Āyatullāh ʿAbd Allāh Jawādī, *Adab Finā' al-Muqaribān*, Vol. 6, p. 326-329.

*﴾Indeed God desires to repel all impurity from you,
O People of the Household, and purify you with
a thorough purification﴿*[83]

2. The highest stage of the Noble Qur'ān is only available to the purified, and that is no other than the Ahl al-Bayt ﷵ:

﴿إِنَّهُ لَقُرْآنٌ كَرِيمٌ﴾

﴾'innahū la-qur'ānun karīm[un]*﴿*

﴿فِي كِتَابٍ مَكْنُونٍ﴾

﴾fī kitābin maknūni[n]*﴿*

﴿لَا يَمَسُّهُ إِلَّا الْمُطَهَّرُونَ﴾

﴾lā yamassuhū 'illā l-muṭahharūn[a]*﴿*

﴿تَنْزِيلٌ مِنْ رَبِّ الْعَالَمِينَ﴾

﴾tanzīlun min rabbi l-ʿālamīn[a]*﴿*

---

[83] Sūrat al-Aḥzāb, Verse 33.

﴾This is indeed a Noble Qur'ān, in a guarded Book,—no one touches it except the pure ones—gradually sent down from the Lord of all the worlds﴿*[84]

3. In addition to confirming that previous heavenly books were sent down, it confirms its superiority over their content.

﴾وَأَنزَلْنَا إِلَيْكَ الْكِتَابَ بِالْحَقِّ مُصَدِّقًا لِمَا بَيْنَ يَدَيْهِ مِنَ الْكِتَابِ وَمُهَيْمِنًا عَلَيْهِ﴿

﴾wa-'anzalnā 'ilayka l-kitāba bi-l-ḥaqqi muṣaddiqan li-mā bayna yadayhi mina l-kitābi wa-muhayminan 'alayhi﴿

﴾We have sent down to you the Book with the truth, confirming what was before it of the Book and as a guardian over it﴿[85]

4. Each prophet's existential stature corresponds to the revelations they received. This means that every prophet possesses comprehensive knowledge of their respective book and a level of understanding on par with that book.

---

[84] Sūrat al-Wāqi'ah, Verses 77-80.

* That is, the Preserved Tablet.

[85] Sūrat al-Mā'idah, Verse 48.

5. Given the significance of the Noble Qur'ān and its precedence over other divine scriptures, coupled with the fact that the Ahl al-Bayt ﷺ have a thorough understanding of the Noble Qur'ān[86], it can be inferred that they, especially Amīr al-Mu'minīn ﷺ and his counterpart, Sayyidah Fāṭimah ﷺ, hold a higher status than the previous prophets.

f. Ziyārat al-Jāmi'ah al-Kabīrah and the illusion of exaggeration

This ziyārah, taught by Imām 'Alī al-Hādī ﷺ, is considered to be the most comprehensive document highlighting the virtues of the Ahl al-Bayt ﷺ. However, some individuals with limited perspective, reacting to those who exaggerate, were hasty in dismissing this, falling into the trap of understatement and labeling this ziyārah as overstated.

Upon examining this notable work, we find that the style and phrasing of this ziyārah bear a strong resemblance to the Noble Qur'ān and the authentic traditions, including those narrated by Sunnī sources. This makes it plausible to

---

86 This scientific structure is derived from the narration of the two weighty things (thaqalayn); if this were not the case, the two weighty things would conflict with each other.

Āmulī, Āyatullāh 'Abd Allāh Jawādī, *Adab Finā' al-Muqaribān,* Vol. 6, p. 328-329.

affirm its authenticity.[87] Moreover, the texts and virtues of the Ahl al-Bayt ﷺ mentioned in this ziyārah echo other prayers and ziyārāt associated with these sacred figures. Considering the infallibility of the tradition's originators, the Prophet ﷺ and Imāms ﷺ, the chance of exaggeration in their words is entirely dismissed.

In Ziyārat al-Jāmiʿah al-Kabīrah, only a fraction of the perfections of these pure luminaries is depicted, while in reality, the virtues of these sacred entities are far more profound. When articulating the supreme virtues of the Ahl al-Bayt ﷺ, there is not the slightest hint of exaggeration. Indeed, just as the qualities of divine perfection are infinite, so are the perfections of these splendid reflections of divinity without end. Amīr al-Mu'minīn ﷺ says:

> "Do not call us 'God.' You may express your admiration for us in any manner you choose. However, you will not reach the reality of our divine attributes, bestowed upon us by God ﷻ, or even a tenth of it, because we are signs, evidence, proofs, representatives, trustees, leaders, faces, eyes, and tongues of God ﷻ."[88]

---

[87] Āmulī, Āyatullāh 'Abd Allāh Jawādī, *Adab Finā' al-Muqaribān,* Vol. 6, p. 330-331.

[88] Al-'Alawī, Muḥammad b. 'Alī b. Ḥusayn, *Al-Manāqib,* p. 74-75.

Majlisī, 'Allamah Muḥammad Bāqir, *Biḥār al-Anwār,* Vol. 26, p. 6.

The only restriction in exaggerating regarding the Ahl al-Bayt 🖈 is not to remove them from the realm of God's ﷻ servitude. Apart from this, there are no boundaries in praising them or expressing their exalted status and virtues, and such expressions can never be overstated.[89]

Miracles and Extraordinary Actions

A sign of attaining the status of guardianship is that the outward nature of things falls under the influence and will of that person. By gaining control over this nature, the guardian can produce extraordinary effects and miracles; if he prays for something, it will happen.

A mu'jizah (miracle), is an act carried out by a prophet as proof of their prophethood. At the same time, a karāmat is an extraordinary event or action unique to those close friends of God ﷻ.[90] Both mu'jizah and karāmat are rooted in the creational [91] authority of the Prophets 🖈 or Imāms 🖈. The distinction between them is that a mu'jizah is associated with a challenge or a claim to prophethood,

---

[89] Āmulī, Āyatullāh 'Abd Allāh Jawādī, *Adab Finā' al-Muqaribān*, Vol. 1, p. 81.

[90] Āmulī, Āyatullāh 'Abd Allāh Jawādī, *Wilāyat dar Qur'ān*, p. 121.

[91] *Wilāyah Takwīniyyah* refers to the creational authority involving direct influence and governance over all aspects of the created world. General examples of this authority can be seen in human abilities such as walking, climbing, or carrying heavy objects.

while a karāmat is not.[92] As a result, some acts of karāmat were also performed by the Prophet himself, such as the collapse of the Arch of Ctesiphon, the drying of the Saveh lake[93], the extinguishing of the fire temple, and the occasion when the rocks greeted the prophet. These events occurred prior to the Holy Prophet's prophethood and were based on his special relationship with God and his future prophetic mission.[94]

Some question the accounts of karāmat from the infallible Ahl al-Bayt, especially those related to Sayyidah Fāṭimah. The main point of contention is that if an extraordinary act or karāmat is carried out by the Ahl al-Bayt, it could lead to confusion, as it might seem that a miracle has lost its uniqueness, making it challenging to differentiate between a prophet and a non-prophet.

The resolution to this uncertainty is that the distinction between the two lies in the fact that one serves as a challenge and justification for prophethood. Those who do not attain divine authority are denied karāmat, and those

---

92 Dukhīm, Samīḥ, *Mawū'at Muṣṭalaḥāt 'Ilm al-Kalām al-Islām*, Vol. 2, p. 1061.

93 According to some narrations, this was a lake located near the city of Saveh, Irān, which is said to have dried up on the night of the birth of Prophet Muḥammad.

94 'Allāmah Ḥillī, Ḥasan b. Yūsuf, *Kashf al-Murād*, p. 352-353.

Āmulī, Āyatullāh 'Abd Allāh Jawādī, *Adab Finā' al-Muqaribān*, Vol. 6, p. 324.

with authority can only achieve this status by following the Prophet ﷺ. Hence, the bearer of karāmat is obedient to the Prophet ﷺ and acknowledges his prophethood, never challenging it. Consequently, it is feasible for karāmat to manifest from someone other than a prophet, and the strongest argument for this is historical evidence. This is cited in numerous traditions and accounts, which testify to the virtues and elevated status of these intimate friends of God ﷻ, who, although not prophets, performed acts of karāmat, like Āṣif b. Barkhiyā.[95]

---

[95] Āmulī, Āyatullāh 'Abd Allāh Jawādī, *Wilāyat dar Qur'ān,* p. 122-123.

Virtues of Sayyidah Fāṭimah

It might be assumed that Sayyidah Fāṭimah attained her esteemed rank and status due to her unique relationship with her father and that Amīr al-Mu'minīn and the rest of the Ahl al-Bayt achieved their positions because of their status. However, the truth is that all these ranks and perfections were attained due to the existence of this sacred lady, not because of her relationship with the Prophet, as others were as close or perhaps closer to him in relation but did not attain this status. Being the wife of Amīr al-Mu'minīn or the mother of the Imāms is also not the reason for her status and virtues because even though Fāṭimah b. Asad was the mother of all twelve Imāms; her status can never be compared with that of Sayyidah Fāṭimah.

Imām Ja'far al-Ṣādiq spoke of this holy woman, stating that she was called 'radiant' because her home and place of worship illuminated brightly for the celestial beings.[96] Sayyidah Fāṭimah is the queen of all women across all realms, and no one in her time was her equal, except for Imām 'Alī. This status pertains to her inherent perfection, not her external familial ties. On her spiritual path, this distinguished lady has ascended to such a level that only the Ahl al-Bayt can comprehend her stature and honor.[97]

---

[96] Ṣadūq, Shaykh Muḥammad b. 'Alī, *Ma'ānī al-Akhbār,* p. 64.

Majlisī, 'Allamah Muḥammad Bāqir, *Biḥār al-Anwār,* Vol. 43, p. 12.

[97] Āmulī, Āyatullāh 'Abd Allāh Jawādī, *'Īd Wilāyat,* p. 113-114.

A Heavenly Gift[98]

Numerous accounts suggest that Sayyidah Fāṭimah ﷺ was conceived from a heavenly fruit during the initial phase of her terrestrial existence. One such account is cited by Shaykh Ṣadūq ﷺ, where Imām ʿAlī al-Riḍā ﷺ quotes the Prophet ﷺ:

> "During the Miʿrāj, Jibrāʾīl took my hand and guided me to heaven. He offered me a heavenly beverage which transformed into a sperm cell within my body. Upon my return to earth, I slept with Khadījah, leading to her pregnancy with Fāṭimah."[99]

In order for Sayyidah Fāṭimah ﷺ, with her lofty status, to descend to earth, a unique foundation was needed. The Prophet ﷺ prepared for the granting of this extraordinary gift by isolating himself and praying for forty days. The significance of this act is highlighted by the fact that Prophet Musā ﷺ undertook a similar process to ready himself for receiving the Torah.[100] Even before this,

---

[98] Āmulī, Āyatullāh ʿAbd Allāh Jawādī, *Sarchishmah Andīshah.*

[99] Ṣadūq, Shaykh Muḥammad b. ʿAlī, *al-Amālī,* p. 461.

Majlisī, ʿAllamah Muḥammad Bāqir, *Biḥār al-Anwār,* Vol. 8, p. 119.

[100] al-Qummī, ʿAlī b. Ibrāhīm, *Tafsīr al-Qummī,* Vol. 1, p. 239.

Majlisī, ʿAllamah Muḥammad Bāqir, *Biḥār al-Anwār,* Vol. 13, p. 213.

Prophet Muḥammad ﷺ had engaged in numerous forms of worship and would frequently visit the cave of Ḥirā, particularly during the sacred month of Ramaḍān, to ready his heart for divine revelation. However, he was tasked with extended periods of worship to achieve the level of preparedness necessary for the arrival of Sayyidah Fāṭimah ؑ.

ʿAllāmah Majlisī narrates that one day, the esteemed Prophet of Islām ﷺ was seated on the land of Abṭaḥ, accompanied by ʿAmār, Mundhar b. Ḍaḥḍāḥ, Abū Bakr, ʿUmar, ʿAbbās, and Imām ʿAlī ؑ. Jibrāʾīl ؑ appeared to the Prophet ﷺ and conveyed God's ﷻ greetings, instructing him to abstain from Sayyidah Khadījah ؑ for forty days. Upon the completion of forty days, Jibrāʾīl ؑ reappeared and relayed God's ﷻ message:

> "Prepare yourself to receive a [divine] gift."

When the Prophet ﷺ inquired about the gift, Jibrāʾīl ؑ replied,

> "I do not know the gift."

Subsequently, Mīkāʾīl ؑ descended with a dish, and the Prophet ﷺ broke his fast with the food from the dish. Then Jibrāʾīl ؑ told the Prophet ﷺ,

> "God ﷻ swears by His nature that He will create a virtuous offspring from your heart tonight."[101]

In another narration, it says,

> "Oh Prophet of God! Tonight, skip your recommended prayers and hurry to Khadījah's house! Because God ﷻ has willed that a pure child is born from your offspring."[102]

Per this decree, the radiance of Fāṭimah ﷺ was moved from the core of her father ﷺ to the womb of her mother.

After some time, Jibrā'īl ﷺ gave the Prophet ﷺ the good news:

> "Oh, Messenger of God! The child in the womb of Khadījah is a precious girl from whom your generation will be born. She is the mother of Imāms and leading

---

[101] al-Shāmī, Shaykh Muḥammad b. Yūsuf al-Ṣāliḥī, *al-Dur al-Naẓīm fī Manāqib al-A'imah*.

[102] Majlisī, 'Allamah Muḥammad Bāqir, *Biḥār al-Anwār*, Vol. 16, p. 79.

figures of religion who will succeed you after the completion of the revelation."[103]

Conversing with her mother during pregnancy

During her time in the womb, Sayyidah Fāṭimah ﷺ would communicate with her mother, Sayyidah Khadījah ﷺ, who narrated:

> "During my pregnancy with Fāṭimah, I experienced a lightness, and she would frequently converse with me from within."[104]

One day, the Prophet ﷺ approached Sayyidah Khadījah ﷺ and noticed that she was conversing with someone, even though no one else was present. He inquired,

> "Who are you speaking with?" She responded, "With the one in my womb." The Prophet ﷺ then said, "Congratulations, Oh Khadījah! She is a girl whom God ﷻ has destined to be the mother of eleven of my

---

[103] Ṣadūq, Shaykh Muḥammad b. 'Alī, *al-Amālī*, p. 593-594.

al-Ṭabarī, Muḥammad b. Jarīr, *Dalā'il al-Imāmat*, p. 77.

Majlisī, 'Allamah Muḥammad Bāqir, *Biḥār al-Anwār*, Vol. 43, p. 2.

[104] ash-Shāfi'ī, 'Abd ur-Raḥman, *Nuzhat al-Majālis*, Vol. 2, p. 321.

> successors who will emerge [as Imāms] after me and their father."[105]

Midwifery of heavenly maids

As Sayyidah Khadījah ﷺ began her labor, she sought the comfort of the women from Quraysh and Banū Ḥāshim, as is customary for women in labor. However, they refused her plea, citing her marriage to Muḥammad ﷺ, the orphan of Abū Ṭālib, who was poor and without wealth, as their reason for not assisting her. This left Sayyidah Khadījah ﷺ in despair. Subsequently, four tall, dark women appeared to her, resembling women from Banū Ḥāshim.

Startled by their presence, one of the women reassured her,

> "Do not grieve, Oh Khadījah, for we are your sisters, messengers from your Lord. I am Sāra, this is Āsiya b. Mazaḥim, your friend in Paradise, this is Maryam b. 'Imrān and this is Kulthūm, the sister of Mūsā b. 'Imrān. God ﷻ sent us to comfort you in the same way women comfort each other."

They positioned themselves around her, one to her right, one to her left, one in front of her, and one behind her. Sayyidah Fāṭimah ﷺ was then born, pure and cleansed. Upon her birth, a light emanated from her that illuminated the houses of Makkah (Mecca), reaching every corner of

---

[105] Shūshtarī, Qāẓī Nūrallāh, *Iḥqāq al-Ḥaqq wa Izhāq al-Bāṭil*, Vol. 10, p. 12.

the East and the West. Ten heavenly maids [ḥūr al-ʿayn] with dark eyes entered, each carrying a pan and a pitcher from Paradise filled with water from al-Kawthar. They handed the pitchers to the woman in front of her, who bathed Sayyidah Fāṭimah ﷺ with the water of al-Kawthar. Following this, she placed her in a cloth whiter than milk, with a fragrance surpassing that of musk and ambergris.[106]

The radiant light during her birth

When the radiant star, Sayyidah Fāṭimah ﷺ, graced this earth with her presence, a light radiated from her magnificence. This light enveloped all the homes in Makkah, leaving no place in the east or west of the world untouched by its brilliance. As mentioned in a narration from Imām Jaʿfar al-Ṣādiq ﷺ:

> "At the time when she [Fāṭimah] was born, a light radiated from her... Certain dwellers of the heavens were proclaiming the birth of Fāṭimah to others, and an exceptionally brilliant light emerged in the sky, a spectacle that the angels had never witnessed

---

[106] Ṣadūq, Shaykh Muḥammad b. ʿAlī, *al-Amālī,* p. 594.

Majlisī, ʿAllamah Muḥammad Bāqir, *Biḥār al-Anwār,* Vol. 43, p. 2-3.

Ibn Shahrāshūb, Muḥammad b. ʿAlī, *Manāqib Āl Abī Ṭālib,* Vol. 2, p. 340.

> before."[107] It is also stated in Sunnī traditions: "At the time of the delivery of Fāṭimah, when Khadījah had given birth to her, the light of her beauty lit up the space."[108]

At the moment of her birth, bowing down to God[109], testifying to His Oneness, His messenger, and the authority of the Ahl al-Bayt were all characteristics that marked the arrival of a distinctive lady into this world.[110] These traits signify that she is destined to fulfill a unique role in the universe.

Naming Fāṭimah

Numerous accounts shed light on the reasoning behind the naming of Sayyidah Fāṭimah. It is said that the name was selected by God Himself. Therefore, the Prophet named her Fāṭimah to signify to the world that she is

---

107 Ṣadūq, Shaykh Muḥammad b. ʿAlī, *al-Amālī,* p. 594.

Majlisī, ʿAllamah Muḥammad Bāqir, *Biḥār al-Anwār,* Vol. 43, p. 3.

108 al-Miṣrī, Shaykh Shuʿayb, *al-Rawḍ al-Faʾiq,* p. 214.

109 Qundūzī, Sulaymān b. Ibrāhīm, *Yanābīʿ al-Mawaddah lī-Dhawī l-Qūrbā,* p. 594-595.

Biyāḍī, ʿAlī b. Yūnus, *al-Ṣirāt al-Mustaqīm*, Vol. 1, p. 170.

110 Ṣadūq, Shaykh Muḥammad b. ʿAlī, *al-Amālī,* p. 594-595.

Majlisī, ʿAllamah Muḥammad Bāqir, *Biḥār al-Anwār,* Vol. 43, p. 3.

devoid of evil,[111] and her genuine Shiʿah are safeguarded from hellfire under her protection.[112] The adversaries of Islām, driven by their greed, are denied the privilege of partaking in this inheritance of the Prophet ﷺ[113] and the wisdom imparted by this nurturing mother.

In one of these narrations, the Holy Prophet ﷺ shared:

> "Jibrāʾīl presented me with an apple from heaven, within which God ﷻ had concealed the light of Fāṭimah, and said,
>
> > 'This apple, a heavenly gift, is sent to you by God ﷻ.'
>
> I received the apple and held it close to my chest. Jibrāʾīl instructed me,
>
> > 'Consume the apple.'

---

[111] Ṣadūq, Shaykh Muḥammad b. ʿAlī, *al-Amālī*, p. 592.

Majlisī, ʿAllamah Muḥammad Bāqir, *Biḥār al-Anwār*, Vol. 43, p. 10.

[112] Ṣadūq, Shaykh Muḥammad b. ʿAlī, *ʿUyūn Akhbār al-Riḍā*, Vol. 2, p. 73.

Majlisī, ʿAllamah Muḥammad Bāqir, *Biḥār al-Anwār*, Vol. 43, p. 12-14.

[113] Ṣadūq, Shaykh Muḥammad b. ʿAlī, *ʿIlal al-Sharāiʿ*, Vol. 1, p. 178.

As I broke open the apple, a light emerged that surprised me. Jibrāʾīl queried,

'Why do you hesitate? Eat without fear, for this is the light of the one known as Manṣūrah in the heavens and Fāṭimah on earth.'

When I asked,

'Why?'

He responded,

'Because on earth, she will rescue her Shīʿah from the fires of hell and sever her enemies from her love. She will aid her devotees in the heavens, as God ⁂ declares:

'On that day, the faithful will rejoice at God's ⁂ help. He helps whomever He wishes...'"[114]

Imām Mūsā b. Jaʿfar ⁂ explains the reason behind the name selection in this manner:

"God ⁂ was aware that numerous tribes would harbor jealousy. Consequently, upon her birth, He named her Fāṭimah, as He proclaimed that the caliphate would reside in the lineage of Fāṭimah's spouse and offspring.

---

[114] Ṣadūq, Shaykh Muḥammad b. ʿAlī, *Maʿānī al-Akhbār*, p. 396-397.

> Thus, her arrival into the world ended the envy others held concerning the caliphate."[115]

Similarly, Imām Muḥammad al-Bāqir ﷺ said,

> "Upon the birth of Sayyidah Nisā', God ﷻ dispatched an angel who instructed the Prophet to name her 'Fāṭimah.' The angel then spoke to her, saying,
>
> > 'I have severed the ties of ignorance from the knowledge within you and have also eliminated menstruation from your being.'"[116]

Other names and titles

Each name and title attributed to Sayyidah Fāṭimah ﷺ encapsulates a portion of her profound existence and radiant character. Thus, understanding these names can serve as a concise and dependable resource for gaining insight into aspects of her existential dimensions.

Due to the Prophet's ﷺ unique perfection across multiple facets, he has been given various names and titles. Each encapsulates and presents a facet of his unparalleled truth.

---

[115] Ṣadūq, Shaykh Muḥammad b. 'Alī, *'Ilal al-Sharāi'*, Vol. 1, p. 178.

[116] Ibid., p. 179.

Imām Ja'far al-Ṣādiq ﷺ has said,

"God ﷻ has nine names for Sayyidah Fāṭimah:

1. Fāṭimah (Distanced from evil, far removed from hellfire, separated from ignorance, devoid of menstruation, shattering the disbeliever's aspiration for the prophet's inheritance...)
2. Ṣadīqah (Profoundly truthful)
3. Mubārakah (Abundantly blessed)
4. Ṭāhirah (Free from impurity)
5. Zakīyyah (Beautiful and redeemed, possessor of goodness and virtue)
6. Rāḍīyyah (Content with God ﷻ)
7. Marḍīyyah (Pleasing to the Divine)
8. Muḥaditha (The one with whom the angels converse)
9. Zahrā' (Enlightening the inhabitants of heaven and earth)."[117]

---

[117] Ṣadūq, Shaykh Muḥammad b. 'Alī, *'Ilal al-Sharāi'*, Vol. 1, p. 178.

Majlisī, 'Allamah Muḥammad Bāqir, *Biḥār al-Anwār*, Vol. 43, p. 10.

In discussions about her titles, often reflective of her virtues and status, it is important to note that there are numerous references in Qur'ānic matter and authentic narrations. Here, we briefly list some of them:

1. Kawthar (One abundant in goodness and blessings)
2. Muṭahhirah (One purified from all impurities)
3. Maḥbūbah (One cherished and loved by God ﷻ)
4. Shafīʿah (Intercessor on the Day of Judgement)
5. Fahīmah (One with high discernment and understanding)
6. Ḥakīmah (One filled with wisdom)
7. Ṣābirah (One patient in the face of hardships)
8. Manṣūrah (One aided by God ﷻ)
9. Maymūnah (One who is a wellspring of goodness and blessings)
10. Ṣafīyyah (One chosen by God ﷻ)
11. Mumtaḥinah (One tested and triumphant in divine trials)
12. Karīmah (One who is kind and dignified)

13. ʿAlīmah (One who is wise and knowledgeable)

14. Raḥīmah (One who is exceedingly kind and heartwarming)

15. Salīmah (One free from any defect)

16. Sharīfah (One with a distinguished status and honor)

17. Maʿṣūmah (One who is infallible from every sin and error)

18. Shahīdah (One who sacrifices her life in the way of God ﷻ while defending the authority of the Imām ﷺ)

Conversing with Divine Angels[118]

Muḥaddath is defined as:

> "Those who can hear the voices of angels, yet are unable to see them."[119]

Consequently, those who hear the angelic words and hold no doubts about them are called Muḥaddath. As per the narrations, just as Maryam ﷺ communicated with angels,

---

[118] Āmulī, Āyatullāh ʿAbd Allāh Jawādī, *Sīrat Payāmbarān dar Qur'ān,* Vol. 7, p. 373.

[119] Ṣaffār, Muḥammad b. Ḥassan, *Baṣā'ir al-Darajāt,* Vol. 1, p. 370.

Majlisī, ʿAllamah Muḥammad Bāqir, *Biḥār al-Anwār,* Vol. 26, p. 76.

one of the significant virtues of Sayyidah Fāṭimah ﷺ was her ability to converse with angels. This is why she was given the name Muḥaddathah.[120]

Imām Jaʿfar al-Ṣādiq ﷺ has said:

> "Fāṭimah was named Muḥaddathah because the angels would descend from the sky to her and would converse with her as they did with Maryam."

He ﷺ further narrated:

> "One evening, Ṣadīqah asked the angels,
>
> > 'Is not Maryam b. ʿImrān the woman who is superior to all others?'
>
> They responded,
>
> > 'No, as Maryam was only the mistress of the women in her era. However, God ﷻ has designated you as the mistress of all women in your era, during Maryam's time, and throughout all times, past and future.'"[121]

---

[120] Ṣadūq, Shaykh Muḥammad b. ʿAlī, *ʿIlal al-Sharāiʿ*, Vol. 1, p. 182.

Majlisī, ʿAllamah Muḥammad Bāqir, *Biḥār al-Anwār*, Vol. 14, p. 206.

[121] Ibid.

He ﷺ went on to say:

> "Fāṭimah's life did not extend beyond 75 days following the Prophet's demise, her heart burdened with profound sorrow for her father. As a result, Jibrā'īl frequently visited her to offer solace in her father's mourning. He would often enlighten her about her father's status and sometimes the events destined to transpire after his passing. Amīr al-Mu'minīn would regularly record these revelations, and this compilation later came to be known as Muṣḥaf Fāṭimah."[122]

In the texts of ziyārah of Sayyidah Fāṭimah ﷺ, we also find:

> "Peace be upon you, oh Muḥaddathah al-'Alīmah."[123]

---

[122] Kulaynī, Shaykh Muḥammad b. Ya'qūb, *al-Kāfī,* Vol. 1, p. 241.

Majlisī, 'Allamah Muḥammad Bāqir, *Biḥār al-Anwār,* Vol. 43, p. 195.

[123] Ṭūsī, Shaykh Muḥammad b. Ḥasan, *Miṣbāḥ al-Mutahajjid wa Silāḥ al-Muta'abbid,* p. 711.

At the Miḥrāb

During prayer, Sayyidah Fāṭimah was so immersed in the Greatness of God, and she disappeared in His Glory that she would begin to tremble.[124]

Regarding her worship and devotion, the Prophet states:

> "When Zahrā' takes her place at the miḥrāb, she shines for the angels in the heavens like a star.
>
> God addresses the angels, saying:
>
> 'Oh angels! Behold my finest servant, Fāṭimah. She stands in My presence, her entire essence quivering in awe of Me, and she has devoted herself to worship Me with complete heart and soul.'"[125]

Ḥasan Baṣrī narrates:

> "You cannot find a more devout person amongst the Muslim nation than Fāṭimah, as when she would

---

[124] al-Ḥillī, Aḥmad b. Fahd, *'Uddat al-Dā'ī wa Najāḥ al-Sā'ī,* p. 151.

Majlisī, 'Allamah Muḥammad Bāqir, *Biḥār al-Anwār,* Vol. 67, p. 400.

[125] Majlisī, 'Allamah Muḥammad Bāqir, *Biḥār al-Anwār,* Vol. 43, p. 172.

worship, it would be to such an extent that her feet would swell."[126]

Imām ʿAlī ﷺ saw her crying on the night of her wedding. When he asked why, she replied,

> "I was thinking about my situation and remembered the end of life and my grave. My relocation from my father's house to my [new] house reminded me of my grave. I swear to you by God ﷻ, let us come and begin our life together with prayer and spend tonight in worship of God ﷻ."[127]

Once, Sayyidah Fāṭimah ﷺ asked her father about those who take their prayers lightly. The Prophet ﷺ said:

> "My dear Fāṭimah! If any man or woman considers prayers light, God ﷻ will inflict fifteen calamities on them. Six worldly calamities, three at the time of death, three calamities in the grave, and three at their resurrection. The six worldly calamities are: God ﷻ removes the blessings from their lifespan, he removes blessings from their day, the light of righteousness from his face fades, he does not reward his [good] actions, his

---

[126] Ibn Shahrāshūb, Muḥammad b. ʿAlī, *Manāqib Āl Abī Ṭālib,* Vol. 3, p. 341.

Majlisī, ʿAllamah Muḥammad Bāqir, *Biḥār al-Anwār,* Vol. 43, p. 84.

[127] Shahīd ath-Thālith, Shūshtarī, Qāḍi Nūr Allāh, *Iḥqāq al-Ḥaqq wa Izhāq al-Bāṭil,* Vol. 23, p. 489.

prayer does not reach the skies, and he does not benefit from the righteous. The three calamities at the time of death are: He leaves the world humiliated, dies in starvation, and dies while thirsty, even if given the water of all the rivers. The three calamities in the grave: God ﷻ will place an angel in his grave who will torment him, the grave will become narrow, and he is consumed with the darkness of the grave. Three calamities on the day of Judgement: God ﷻ will assign a custodian to him who will execute him while his face is on the ground and others are observing. His judgment will be determined with hardship, and God ﷻ will withhold His mercy from him, leading to his perpetual punishment."[128]

The Eternal Mistress of the Women of the World

The Prophet ﷺ conveys to Imām ʿAlī ؑ:

"I envision the day of Judgement when my daughter, Fāṭimah ؑ, will step into a radiant aura. She will be accompanied by seventy thousand angels on her right, seventy thousand on her left, seventy thousand angels behind her, and seventy thousand angels in front of

---

[128] Sayyid ʿAlī b. Mūsā b. Jaʿfar b. Ṭāwūs (Ibn Ṭāwūs), *Falāḥ al-Sāʾil wa Najāḥ al-Masāʾil*, p. 22.

Majlisī, ʿAllamah Muḥammad Bāqir, *Biḥār al-Anwār*, Vol. 80, p. 21-22.

her. Certainly, Fāṭimah is the best of all women in the world."

Amīr al-Mu'minīn ﷺ asked,

"Is Fāṭimah the best of women of her time only?"

He ﷺ replied:

"That status is reserved for Maryam while my daughter, Fāṭimah, is the best of all women in the world from the beginning to its end. Whenever Fāṭimah stands for worship, seventy thousand angels greet her. In the same way that Maryam was addressed, they greet Fāṭimah and say:

> 'Oh Fāṭimah! God chose you and He made you pure and gave you superiority over all the women of the world.'"[129]

Ibn 'Abbās narrates that the Prophet ﷺ has said,

"I hold the highest rank among the Prophets, messengers, and even the archangels. My successors are the best successors of the Prophets. My progeny is superior to the progeny of the prophets and messengers [before me]. My companions – who follow my path – are better than the companions of the prophets and

---

[129] Ṣadūq, Shaykh Muḥammad b. 'Alī, *al-Amālī,* p. 486-487.

messengers [before me]. My daughter, Fāṭimah, is the mistress of the women of the world."[130]

God's ﷻ Chosen One

In the final will of the Prophet ﷺ to Amīr al-Mu'minīn ﷺ, he says:

> "Oh 'Alī! Upon God's ﷻ first gaze at the world, He selected me. When He cast His second glance, you were His choice. At His third look, He picked the Imāms from your offspring. And when He looked for the fourth time, Fāṭimah was chosen among all women."[131]

The Counterpart of the Noble Qur'ān[132]

The Prophet of Islām ﷺ introduces two precious legacies to guide his people after his departure:

---

130 Ibid., p. 298.

Majlisī, 'Allamah Muḥammad Bāqir, *Biḥār al-Anwār,* Vol. 8, p. 22.

131 Ṣadūq, Shaykh Muḥammad b. 'Alī, *al-Khiṣāl,* Vol. 1, p. p. 206-207.

132 Āmulī, Āyatullāh 'Abd Allāh Jawādī, *Sharī'at dar Āyinah Ma'rifat,* p. 144.

"I will leave amongst you two weighty things, the book of God 🌿 and my progeny."[133]

The Prophet 🌿 has established the Noble Qur'ān and his progeny as the guiding principles of Islāmic law for his followers after his demise. Their flawless guidance is a comprehensive and clear model for humanity to emulate. Their words and deeds align with the Noble Qur'ān's teachings, setting the morality standard. Thus, adherence to the Ahl al-Bayt 🌿 traditions is regarded as the most accurate explanation and interpretation of the Noble Qur'ān's verses, forming an integral part of Islāmic law. The Ahl al-Bayt 🌿 serves as a reference or condition for the generalities and absolutes within the verses. Therefore, partial adherence to this Islāmic law equates to abandoning all divine revelation and guidance, as it neglects its conditions. Hence, to truly embrace the Noble Qur'ān is to embrace the traditions and lineage of Prophet Muḥammad 🌿, Sayyidah Fāṭimah 🌿, and the twelve infallible leaders 🌿, who have always been and will always be inseparable from the Noble Qur'ān following the Prophet's 🌿 death. This is why Sayyidah Fāṭimah's 🌿 speech, character, love, and hatred, which mirror the Noble

---

[133] Ṣadūq, Shaykh Muḥammad b. ʿAlī, *al-Amālī*, p. 415.

Majlisī, ʿAllamah Muḥammad Bāqir, *Biḥār al-Anwār*, Vol. 24, p. 124.

Qur'ān, embody the Islāmic law and are indeed equivalent to the love and hatred of God ﷻ.[134]

A Standard for God's ﷻ Pleasure or Anger[135]

The Prophet ﷺ is affirmed by the Qur'ān to be the voice of God ﷻ. His actions, speech, silence, and emotions reflect God's ﷻ Will. As stated in the Noble Qur'ān,

﴿وَما يَنطِقُ عَنِ الهَوىٰ﴾

﴿*wa-mā yanṭiqu ʿani l-hawā*﴾

﴿*Nor does he speak out of [his own] desire*﴾[136]

[134] Āmulī, Āyatullāh ʿAbd Allāh Jawādī, *Sharīʿat dar Āyinah Maʿrifat,* p. 144.

[135] Āmulī, Āyatullāh ʿAbd Allāh Jawādī, *Sarchishmah Andīshah,* Vol. 2, p. 85.

[136] Sūrat an-Najm, Verse 3.

And regarding Sayyidah Fāṭimah ﷺ, he ﷺ says:

> "Fāṭimah is part of me; her happiness is my happiness, and her anger is my anger."[137]

He ﷺ also says:

> "God ﷻ is angered when Fāṭimah is angered, and pleased when she is pleased."[138]

If individuals are not free from impurity or desire, their contentment cannot be a benchmark for truth. Whether their current satisfaction signifies God's ﷻ pleasure or their momentary anger reflects God's ﷻ Wrath remains uncertain. Conversely, if a person is flawless and devoid of desire and lust, their joy and anger undoubtedly become a standard for discerning right from wrong. Such a perfect individual embodies God's ﷻ Pleasure and is a reference for evaluating one's deeds.

---

137 Al-Amīn, Sayyid Muḥsin, *A'yān al-Shī'a,* Vol. 1, p. 307.

Ṣadūq, Shaykh Muḥammad b. 'Alī, *al-Amālī,* p. 104.

Ibn Shahrāshūb, Muḥammad b. 'Alī, *Manāqib Āl Abī Ṭālib,* Vol. 3, p. 332.

138 Ṣadūq, Shaykh Muḥammad b. 'Alī, *Ma'ānī al-Akhbār,* p. 303.

Majlisī, 'Allamah Muḥammad Bāqir, *Biḥār al-Anwār,* Vol. 43, p. 26.

Just as the Prophet 🌸 served as a benchmark for his people's actions, with his joy and wrath reflecting God's 🌸 Pleasure and Anger, Sayyidah Fāṭimah 🌸 held a similar position. Her happiness or displeasure mirrored the Prophet's 🌸 emotions. Her words, deeds, and conduct were infallible, akin to her beliefs, thoughts, and worldview. Like her counterpart, Amīr al-Mu'minīn 🌸, she is a measure of the validity of others' actions and a manifestation of God's 🌸 Pleasure.

The Prophet 🌸 said:

> "'Alī is with the Truth, and the Truth is with him, and it revolves around him wherever he is."[139]

If a being is perfect and all its characteristics align with the axis of truth. Consequently, their joy and wrath are rooted in this axis of truth. This is a testament to the absolute infallibility of Sayyidah Fāṭimah 🌸.[140]

The Prophet 🌸's remarks about Sayyidah Fāṭimah 🌸 were not merely the result of paternal love, as he did not express the same feelings towards his other children, namely Qāsim and Ibrāhīm. Similarly, the Prophet 🌸 demonstrated a unique behavior towards his grandchildren, Imām al-

---

[139] Ibn Shahrāshūb, Muḥammad b. 'Alī, *Manāqib Āl Abī Ṭālib*, Vol. 3, p. 62.

[140] Āmulī, Āyatullāh 'Abd Allāh Jawādī, *Sarchishmah Andīshah*, Vol. 2, p. 85.

Ḥasan and Imām al-Ḥusayn ؑ, that he did not exhibit with his children. Hence, until this is comprehended, one cannot truly grasp the phrase's meaning:

> "Fāṭimah is a part of me."[141] [142]

A Heavenly Woman in Human form[143]

The Prophet ﷺ stated,

> "During my ascension to the sky, Jibrā'īl guided me into heaven, where I was presented with a date, which I consumed. That heavenly date transformed into a sperm cell within me. Upon my return to earth, I was intimate with Khadījah, resulting in her pregnancy with Fāṭimah. Thus, Fāṭimah is a heavenly woman manifested in human form. Whenever I longed for the scent of heaven, I would find it in the fragrance of Fāṭimah."[144]

---

[141] Ṭūsī, Shaykh Muḥammad b. Ḥasan, *al-Amālī,* p. 24.

[142] Āmulī, Āyatullāh 'Abd Allāh Jawādī, *Tasnīm fī Tafsīr al-Qur'ān,* Vol. 17, p. 538.

[143] Ibid., Vol. 8, p. 442.

[144] Ṣadūq, Shaykh Muḥammad b. 'Alī, *al-Amālī,* p. 461.

Majlisī, 'Allamah Muḥammad Bāqir, *Biḥār al-Anwār,* Vol. 8, p. 119.

Imām Ja'far al-Ṣādiq recounts:

"The Prophet ﷺ would frequently kiss Fāṭimah, which would upset 'Ā'ishah. The Prophet ﷺ explained,

'Oh 'Ā'ishah! During my heavenly journey, Jibrā'īl led me to the Ṭūbā tree, and I consumed its fruits. God instilled its essence in my heart, from which Fāṭimah was conceived. Therefore, whenever I yearn for heaven, I kiss Fāṭimah. As I kiss her, I smell the scent of the Ṭūbā tree. Fāṭimah is a heavenly maid embodied in human form.'"[145]

An Intercessor for the Believers[146]

Muḥammad b. Muslim narrates that he heard from Imām Muḥammad al-Bāqir, who stated:

"On the day of judgment, Fāṭimah will position herself at the entrance of hell. On that day, everyone's foreheads will bear the inscription 'infidel or believer.' Then, our friends who have sinned will be summoned

---

[145] al-Ḥuwayzī, al-'Arūsī, *Tafsīr Nūr al-Thaqalayn,* Vol. 2, p. 502.

al-Qummī, 'Alī b. Ibrāhīm, *Tafsīr al-Qummī,* Vol. 1, p. 22.

[146] Āmulī, Āyatullāh 'Abd Allāh Jawādī, *Tasnīm fī Tafsīr al-Qur'ān,* Vol. 4, p. 296.

Āmulī, Āyatullāh 'Abd Allāh Jawādī, *Tafsīr Mauwḍū'ī Qur'ān al-Karīm,* Vol. 5, p. 137.

to enter the hellfire. As they approach hell, Fāṭimah will read 'lovers of the Ahl al-Bayt' on their foreheads. She will cry out:

> 'Oh Lord! You have bestowed upon me the name Fāṭimah, and through me, you have exempted anyone who cherishes me and my children from the hellfire. Your Promise is steadfast, and You never break Your Promise.'

God ﷻ will reply:

> 'Indeed, I have commanded this sinful servant to proceed to hell so that you may intercede for him, and I accept your intercession to reveal your honor and status to the angels, prophets, and all people on the day of resurrection. Whoever's forehead reads 'believer,' guide them by their hands into paradise.'"[147]

Jābir narrates that he once asked Imām Muḥammad al-Bāqir ﷺ:

> "Tell me a narration of the virtues of Fāṭimah al-Zahrā' so that I may narrate it for your Shī'ah."

The Imām ﷺ replied,

---

[147] Ṣadūq, Shaykh Muḥammad b. 'Alī, *'Ilal al-Sharāi'*, Vol. 1, p. 179.

"On the day of Judgement, luminous pulpits will be set for the Messenger of God and other prophets. Then, a command will be issued:

> 'Oh, assembly! Avert your eyes, for Fāṭimah is making her entrance into paradise.'

Subsequently, God ﷻ will station one hundred thousand angels on her right, one hundred thousand on her left, and one hundred thousand will unfold their wings to escort her towards heaven. Upon reaching the gates of heaven, Sayyidah Fāṭimah will pause and survey her surroundings.

God ﷻ will inquire:

> 'Oh, daughter of my confidant! What prompts your hesitation when I have invited you into heaven?'

She responds:

> 'Oh Lord! I wish to be acknowledged on this day.'

God ﷻ declares:

> 'Oh, daughter of my beloved! Return and see that whoever holds love for you or your children in their heart, take their hand and grant them admission into heaven.'"

Imām Muḥammad al-Bāqir 🌸 proclaimed:

> "By God 🌸, Oh Jābir! On this day, Fāṭimah selects the
> Shīʿah and her admirers as birds choose the finest seeds
> among the poor ones. So, when a Shīʿah arrives at the
> gates of heaven, God 🌸 instills a moment of pause and
> uncertainty in their hearts. When they exhibit
> hesitation, God 🌸 will question:
>
>> 'Oh, my confidant! What causes your hesitation
>> now that Fāṭimah has interceded for you?'
>
> The response will be:
>
>> 'My Lord! I wish for my honor to be recognized on
>> this day.'
>
> God 🌸 will then instruct:
>
>> 'Return and identify those who loved you for
>> Fāṭimah's sake, those who provided you with food
>> and clothing, for Fāṭimah's sake, and those who
>> found you when you were lost, all for the sake of
>> Fāṭimah. Take their hands and guide them into
>> heaven.'"[148]

---

[148] Majlisī, ʿAllamah Muḥammad Bāqir, *Biḥār al-Anwār*,
Vol. 8, p. 51-52.

Furat b. Ibrāhīm, *Tafsīr Furat*, p. 298-299.

The Prophet's ﷺ Fragrant Flower

As suggested by the verses of the Noble Qur'ān, the customs of the ignorant Arab tribes were such that the birth of a baby girl would be met with dismay and resentment. Their faces would darken with disappointment, and they would distance themselves from their community, considering it a disgrace. In some cases, they would even resort to burying the newborn girl alive:

﴿وَإِذَا بُشِّرَ أَحَدُهُم بِالْأُنثَىٰ ظَلَّ وَجْهُهُ مُسْوَدًّا وَهُوَ كَظِيمٌ﴾

﴾*wa-'idhā bushshira 'aḥaduhum bi-l-'unthā ẓalla wajhuhū muswaddan wa-huwa kaẓīm*[un]﴿

﴿يَتَوَارَىٰ مِنَ الْقَوْمِ مِن سُوءِ مَا بُشِّرَ بِهِ ۚ أَيُمْسِكُهُ عَلَىٰ هُونٍ أَمْ يَدُسُّهُ فِي التُّرَابِ ۗ أَلَا سَاءَ مَا يَحْكُمُونَ﴾

﴾*yatawārā mina l-qawmi min sū'i mā bushshira bihī 'a-yumsikuhū 'alā hūnin 'am yadussuhū fī t-turābi 'a-lā sā'a mā yaḥkumūn*[a]﴿

﴾*When one of them is brought the news of a female [newborn], his face becomes darkened and he chokes with suppressed agony. He hides from the people out of distress at the news he has been brought: shall he retain it in* *humiliation, or bury it in the ground!* Look! Evil is the judgement that they make*﴿[149]

This culture of ignorance had penetrated amongst the Arabs so much that even during the time of the Prophet ﷺ, many girls were buried alive for the same reason:

﴿وَإِذَا الْمَوْءُودَةُ سُئِلَتْ﴾

﴿*wa-'idhā l-maw'ūdatu su'ilat*﴾

﴿بِأَيِّ ذَنبٍ قُتِلَتْ﴾

﴿*bi-'ayyi dhanbin qutilat*﴾

﴿*When the girl buried-alive will be asked for what sin she was killed*﴾[150]

Islām challenged this misguided tradition, with the Prophet ﷺ playing a pivotal role in its opposition. For instance, upon the birth of Sayyidah Fāṭimah ﷺ, he

---

149 Sūrat an-Naḥl, Verses 58-59.

* This refers to the practice of pre-Islāmic Arabs of burying their newborn daughters alive.

150 Sūrat at-Takwīr, Verse 8-9.

demonstrated immense respect for her, often seen expressing his affection by kissing her hands.[151]

Whenever he would travel, upon his departure and return, he would visit her.[152]

Imām Jaʿfar al-Ṣādiq 🌸 states:

"Daughters are viewed as virtuous and good deeds, while sons are seen as blessings. Virtuous deeds are rewarded, but blessings are subject to questioning."[153]

He 🌸 further narrates:

"When the Prophet was informed of Fāṭimah's birth, he observed the reactions of his companions. Noticing remnants of the ignorant culture on their faces, he questioned:

[151] al-Irdibillī, ʿAlī b. ʿĪsā Hakkārī, *Kashf al-Ghummah fī Maʿrifat al-Aʾimma*, Vol. 1, p. 454.

[152] Ibn Shahrāshūb, Muḥammad b. ʿAlī, *Manāqib Āl Abī Ṭālib*, Vol. 3, p. 332.

Majlisī, ʿAllamah Muḥammad Bāqir, *Biḥār al-Anwār*, Vol. 43, p. 40.

[153] Ṣadūq, Shaykh Muḥammad b. ʿAlī, *Thawāb al-Aʿmāl*, p. 201-202.

al-Ḥuwayzī, al-ʿArūsī, *Tafsīr Nūr al-Thaqalayn*, Vol. 3, p. 61.

'What is this look I see on your faces? Fāṭimah is a bouquet whose scent I perceive, and her sustenance is in God ﷻ.'"[154] [155]

The Value of Visiting Her

It has been narrated from the Prophet ﷺ:

"God ﷻ has assigned a group of angels to protect Fāṭimah al-Zahrā' from her front, behind, left and right, and to accompany her during her lifetime until her grave and even after death, they send endless blessings on her, her father, her husband, and her children. Whoever visits me after my death is as if he has visited Fāṭimah. Whoever visits Fāṭimah, it is as if he has visited me, and one who visits 'Alī b. Abī Ṭālib, it is as if he has visited Fāṭimah. Whoever visits their progeny, it is as if he has visited them [all]."[156]

---

[154] Ṣadūq, Shaykh Muḥammad b. 'Alī, *Thawāb al-A'māl,* p. 202.

Majlisī, 'Allamah Muḥammad Bāqir, *Biḥār al-Anwār,* Vol. 101, p. 104.

[155] Āmulī, Āyatullāh 'Abd Allāh Jawādī, *Tafsīr Mauwḍū'ī Qur'ān al-Karīm,* Vol. 4, p. 406.

[156] Majlisī, 'Allamah Muḥammad Bāqir, *Biḥār al-Anwār,* Vol. 97, p. 122-123.

al-Ṭabarī, Muḥammad b. 'Alī, *Bishārat al-Muṣṭafā li Shī'at al-Murtaḍā,* p. 139.

Knowledge of the Unseen

Divine revelation can be categorized into two types: legislative and non-legislative. It is worth noting that the Ahl al-Bayt ﷺ would reflect the Prophet ﷺ in terms of legislative revelation, which was exclusive to him. However, the avenue of divine revelation was accessible to them, and they were recipients of numerous truths that served as confirmatory knowledge. As per the verses of the Noble Qur'ān discussing Mubāhalah[157], they are recipients of news and spread it to others. In the following verse, God ﷻ says:

﴿فَمَنْ حَاجَّكَ فِيهِ مِنْ بَعْدِ مَا جَاءَكَ مِنَ الْعِلْمِ فَقُلْ تَعَالَوْا نَدْعُ أَبْنَاءَنَا وَأَبْنَاءَكُمْ وَنِسَاءَنَا وَنِسَاءَكُمْ وَأَنْفُسَنَا وَأَنْفُسَكُمْ ثُمَّ نَبْتَهِلْ فَنَجْعَلْ لَعْنَتَ اللَّهِ عَلَى الْكَاذِبِينَ﴾

﴿fa-man ḥājjaka fīhi min baʿdi mā jāʾaka mina l-ʿilmi fa-qul taʿālaw nadʿu ʾabnāʾanā wa-ʾabnāʾakum wa-nisāʾanā wa-nisāʾakum wa-ʾanfusanā wa-ʾanfusakum thumma nabtahil fa-najʿal laʿnata llāhi ʿalā l-kādhibīna[a]﴾

﴿Should anyone argue with you concerning him, after the knowledge that has come to you, say, 'Come! Let us call our sons and your sons, our women and your women, our souls

---

[157] *Mubāhalah* is derived from its Arabic root 'blah,' meaning 'curse.' Thus, the act of al-Mubāhalah means that each of the two parties invokes the curse of God on the other; if the latter is untruthful.

and your souls, then let us pray earnestly and call down God's curse upon the liars'[158] [159]

During the challenge of Mubāhalah, the language used was plural rather than singular: "*Then let us pray earnestly, and call down God's curse upon the liars.*"[160] This implies both parties have a claim, either truthful and the other lying, or the reverse. The labels 'truthful' and 'liar' apply to those with the authority to make a statement and have a claim to present. If these two conditions are not fulfilled, the individual is merely an observer without a message to be assessed. It is evident that the Prophet ﷺ, 'Alī b. Abī Ṭālib ﷺ, Sayyidah Fāṭimah ﷺ, and al-Ḥasan and al-Ḥusayn ﷺ are all cognizant of the world's truths, disseminate news to others, and make declarations. Hence, based on this verse's interpretation, Sayyidah Fāṭimah ﷺ was aware of the unseen, and the truth of divine inspiration matters.[161]

---

158 Sūrat Āl 'Imrān, Verse 61.

159 Indeed, if an individual lies about a minor issue, they are not necessarily implicated by the Verse of Mubāhalah. While lying is a grave sin, in the context of Mubāhalah, it pertains to divine authority and prophethood.

160 Sūrat Āl 'Imrān, Verse 61.

161 Āmulī, Āyatullāh 'Abd Allāh Jawādī, *'Īd Wilāyat*, p. 77-78.

Her Wilāyat

The position of Imāmate in Islāmic culture

The Messenger of God said in a famous narration:

> "Whoever dies while not knowing the Imām of his time dies in ignorance."[162]

When Imām al-Ḥusayn was asked about the knowledge of God, he said:

> "The knowledge of the people of all times is [to recognize] their Imām, the one who is owed their obedience."[163]

Imām Muḥammad al-Bāqir was asked:

> "Is recognizing the Imām from amongst you obligatory on all people?"

[162] Ibn Shahrāshūb, Muḥammad b. 'Alī, *Manāqib Āl Abī Ṭālib,* Vol. 1, p. 246.

Majlisī, 'Allamah Muḥammad Bāqir, *Biḥār al-Anwār,* Vol. 32, p. 331.

[163] Ṣadūq, Shaykh Muḥammad b. 'Alī, *'Ilal al-Sharāi',* Vol. 1, p. 9.

Majlisī, 'Allamah Muḥammad Bāqir, *Biḥār al-Anwār,* Vol. 23, p. 83.

The Imām replied:

> "God selected the Prophet Muḥammad from amongst all the people. Whoever believes in and follows God and Muḥammad, he must recognize the Imām from amongst us."[164]

Similarly, Imām Muḥammad al-Bāqir has said:

> "Whoever dies without an Imām has left this world in ignorance, and people are not excused unless they recognize the Imām of their time. Whoever recognizes his Imām and dies will not be disadvantaged."[165]

Imām Jaʿfar al-Ṣādiq explains the statement of the Prophet when he was once asked what is meant by the death of ignorance in the words of the Prophet.

He said:

> "Ignorance means disbelief, hypocrisy, and misguidance."[166]

---

164 Kulaynī, Shaykh Muḥammad b. Yaʿqūb, *al-Kāfī,* Vol. 1, p. 180-181.

165 al-Barqī, Aḥmad b. Muḥammad b. Khālid, *al-Maḥāsin,* Vol. 1, p. 155.

Majlisī, ʿAllamah Muḥammad Bāqir, *Biḥār al-Anwār,* Vol. 23, p. 77.

166 Kulaynī, Shaykh Muḥammad b. Yaʿqūb, *al-Kāfī,* Vol. 1, p. 377.

Majlisī, ʿAllamah Muḥammad Bāqir, *Biḥār al-Anwār,* Vol. 8, p. 362.

In another explanation, he 🌸 expanded on this and said:

> "Whoever spends a night without knowing the Imām
> of his time has died the death of ignorance."[167]

The narrations, as cited in the most reliable Shī'ah sources
with different phrasings, emphasize that it is important to
be aware of the Imām and know their names and virtues at
all times. This knowledge is so essential that one should not
pass a night without recognizing his Imām.

This narration has also been mentioned in Sunnī sources in
the same way:

> "Whoever dies while not knowing the Imām of his
> time, dies as an ignorant [person]."[168]

Fakhr Rāḍī narrates that the Prophet 🌸 has said:

> "Whoever dies while not knowing the Imām of his
> time, dies the death of a Jew or Christian (meaning he
> will not die a Muslim)."[169]

---

167 Nu'mānī, Muḥammad b. Ibrāhīm, *Kitāb al-Ghaybah*, p. 127.

168 Qundūzī, Sulaymān b. Ibrāhīm, *Yanābī' al-Mawaddah li-Dhawī
l-Qūrbā*, Vol. 3, p. 372 and 456.

Ibn Abī al-Ḥadīd, *Sharḥ Nahj al-Balāghah*, Vol. 13, p. 242.

169 'Allāmah Ḥillī, Ḥasan b. Yūsuf, Shahīd Thānī, Zayn al-Dīn al-'Amilī
al-Jubā'ī, Mullā Ṣadrā, Muḥammad b. Ibrāhīm, and Ibn
Bābawayh, 'Alī, *Majmū'at al-Rasā'il*, p. 384.

The late ʿAllāmah Amīnī ﵀ brought different narrations of this ḥadīth from Sunnī sources:

1. "He who dies without an Imām, dies the death of ignorance."[170]

2. "He who dies not recognizing his Imām of the time dies the death of ignorance."[171]

3. "He who dies and has no Imām dies the death of ignorance."[172] [173]

Sayyidah Fāṭimah's ﷺ stance on Imāmate

---

[170] Ibn Ḥanbal, Aḥmad, *Musnad Aḥmad b. Ḥanbal,* Vol. 4, p. 96.

al-Ṭayālisī, Abū Dāwūd Sulaymān b. Dāwūd, *Musnad Abī Dawūd al-Ṭayālīsī,* p. 259.

Haythamī, Ḥāfiẓ, *Majmaʿ al-Zawāʾid,* Vol. 5, p. 218.

[171] Taftāzānī, Saʿd al-Dīn, *Sharḥ Maqāṣid,* Vol. 5, p. 239.

Qārī, ʿAlī b. Sultān, *Mirqāt al-Mafātīḥ,* Vol. 6, p. 2398.

[172] Askāfī, Abū Jaʿfar, *al-Miʿyār wal-Muwāzana,* p. 24.

Haythamī, Ḥāfiẓ, *Majmaʿ al-Zawāʾid,* Vol. 5, p. 224.

[173] Amīnī, Shaykh ʿAbdul Ḥusayn Amīnī, *al-Ghadīr fī al-Kitāb wal-Sunna wal-Adab,* Vol. 10, p. 492–494.

Many other narrations were mentioned in this book, but have not been included in this book.

As per the narration mentioned in both Shī'ah and Sunnī sources, a question emerges regarding whether Sayyidah Fāṭimah 🌸 was aware of the Imām of her time. It is utterly inconceivable that someone who is an integral part of the Prophet 🌸 and the spouse of Amīr al-Mu'minīn 🌸 would reject a fundamental aspect of the faith and refrain from acknowledging it. This notion is not logically acceptable.[174] Nor consistent with her infallible nature. The Verse of Purification[175] attests to Sayyidah Fāṭimah's 🌸 immunity from error, and the Prophet's 🌸 words endorse her character.

Throughout history, numerous Sunnī scholars have exhibited a lack of impartiality. Despite their ability to rationalize many aspects of Imāmate while rejecting its acceptance and while justifying the caliphate of the three caliphs following the Prophet 🌸, they are often taken aback when they encounter the conduct of Sayyidah Fāṭimah 🌸 towards the caliphs in their authentic narrations. They either bypass it with a significant silence or yield to the truth of Sayyidah Fāṭimah 🌸.

This question will echo through history until the day of Judgement: To whom did Sayyidah Fāṭimah, the daughter of the Prophet 🌸, pledge her allegiance, and whom did she acknowledge as her Imām? Without a doubt, Sayyidah

---

[174] Idib., p. 495.

[175] Sūrat al-Aḥzāb, Verse 33; this verse will be discussed in detail in the next chapter.

Fāṭimah ؑ did not pledge allegiance to Abū Bakr, as he did not converse with her until her final moments. If she, Imām ʿAlī ؑ, and their companions who were present at Imām ʿAlī's ؑ house had pledged allegiance, they would not have set fire to the door of Sayyidah Fāṭimah's ؑ house.

It is narrated that:

> "Fāṭimah departed from Abū Bakr in anger, remained upset with him, and did not converse with him until her death. ʿAlī prayed for her throughout the night and buried her without informing Abū Bakr to attend her funeral prayer."[176]

Similarly, ʿAbdullāh b. Muslim b. Qutaybah ad-Dīnawarī recounts in his book that Sayyidah Fāṭimah al-Zahrāʾ ؑ, on her deathbed, said to Abū Bakr and ʿUmar:

> "I testify to God ﷻ and the angels that you both upset me and did not seek my contentment. When I see the Prophet, I will complain about both of you."[177]

[176] Muslim b. al-Ḥajjāj, *Ṣaḥīḥ Muslim,* Vol. 5, p. 154.

Bukhārī, Muḥammad b. Ismāʿīl, *Ṣaḥīḥ Bukhārī,* Vol. 5, p. 82.

[177] Dinawarī , ʿAbdullāh b. Muslim b. Qutaybah, *al-Imāmah wa al-Siyāsa,* Vol. 1, p. 20 and 31.

In Shī'ah references, it is mentioned that Sayyidah Fāṭimah ﷺ declared,

> "By God ﷻ, after this point, I will not utter a single word to either of you until I rush to meet God ﷻ. I will present your complaint to Him ﷻ and explain your actions towards me."[178]

Specifically about Abū Bakr, she stated,

> "By God ﷻ, I will never speak with you. I swear to God ﷻ, I will invoke a curse upon you."[179]

Then she said:

> "Oh, Abū Bakr! How quickly you made apparent your secret grudges towards the Ahl al-Bayt of the Prophet ﷺ."

---

[178] Ṣadūq, Shaykh Muḥammad b. 'Alī, *'Ilal al-Sharāi'*, Vol. 1, p. 187.

Majlisī, 'Allamah Muḥammad Bāqir, *Biḥār al-Anwār,* Vol. 43, p. 204.

[179] Baṣrī, Aḥmad b. 'Abd al-'Azīz, *al-Saqīfah wa Fadak,* p. 102.

Amīnī, Shaykh 'Abdul Ḥusayn, *al-Ghadīr fī al-Kitāb wal-Sunna wal-Adab,* Vol. 7, p. 309.

Ṣadūq, Shaykh Muḥammad b. 'Alī, *'Uyūn Akhbār al-Riḍā,* Vol. 1, p. 318.

And she continued:

> "I swear by God, I will not talk to 'Umar for as long as I live."[180]

To address this query, one should look to Sayyidah Fāṭimah 🌸 herself for guidance on who she acknowledges as her Imām and her interpretation of what an Imām is. As soon as she set foot on this earth, she proclaimed:

> "I bear witness that there is no deity but God 🕮, and that my father is God's messenger, the most eminent of all prophets, and that my spouse is the foremost of guardians, and my offspring are the leaders of the Muslim community."[181]

In Uḥud, Sayyidah Fāṭimah al-Zahrā' 🌸 was seen mourning beside Ḥamzah's grave.

---

[180] Baṣrī, Aḥmad b. 'Abd al-'Azīz, *al-Saqīfah wa Fadak*, p. 102.

Majlisī, 'Allāmah Muḥammad Bāqir, *Biḥār al-Anwār*, Vol. 28, p. 322.

Amīnī, Shaykh 'Abdul Ḥusayn, *al-Ghadīr fī al-Kitāb wal-Sunna wal-Adab*, Vol. 7, p. 104.

[181] Ṣadūq, Shaykh Muḥammad b. 'Alī, *al-Amālī*, p. 594-595.

Majlisī, 'Allāmah Muḥammad Bāqir, *Biḥār al-Anwār*, Vol. 43, p. 3.

Maḥmūd b. Labīd asked:

> "Can we derive evidence for 'Alī's Imāmate from the Prophet's words?"

Sayyidah Fāṭimah responded that she had heard the Prophet declare:

> "'Alī is the most deserving among you to be my successor, he is the Imām and caliph after me, and my two sons [al-Ḥasan and al-Ḥusayn] along with nine of al-Ḥusayn's descendants are destined to be the leaders [following him]."[182]

Sayyidah Fāṭimah not only acknowledged and proclaimed the Imāmate of Imām 'Alī, but she did so while grieving the loss of her dear father. Despite her sorrow, her deepest anguish was rooted in the usurpation of Imām 'Alī's rightful caliphate. Umm Salmah recounts that she approached Sayyidah Fāṭimah and inquired:

> "Oh, daughter of the Prophet! How was your night?"

Sayyidah Fāṭimah responded:

---

[182] al-Qummī, 'Alī b. Muḥammad b. 'Alī al-Khazzaz, *Kifāyat al-Athar*, p. 198-199.

Majlisī, 'Allamah Muḥammad Bāqir, *Biḥār al-Anwār*, Vol. 36, p. 352-353.

> "I was engulfed in profound sorrow due to the demise of the Prophet while his successor is being wronged. I solemnly swear to God ﷻ that the curtain of His Sanctity has been ripped apart."[183]

In her continuation of her struggle in supporting the Imām of her time, she wrote on a piece of paper:

> "The nation who broke their covenant to God ﷻ and His Prophet ﷺ regarding Amīr al-Mu'minīn do not have the right to pray [the prayer of the deceased] over me."[184]

Sayyidah Fāṭimah ؑ acknowledged her Imām and defended him verbally and physically, confronting the Imām's enemies until her demise. Ultimately, she gave up her life and attained martyrdom in the pursuit of Imāmate. During the distressing incident when Imām 'Alī ؑ was forcibly taken to the mosque, she cried out:

---

[183] Ibn Shahrāshūb, Muḥammad b. 'Alī, *Manāqib Āl Abī Ṭālib,* Vol. 2, p. 205.

Majlisī, 'Allamah Muḥammad Bāqir, *Biḥār al-Anwār,* Vol. 43, p. 156.

[184] Khuṣaybī, Ḥusayn b. Ḥamadān, *al-Hidāyat al-Kubrā*, p. 178.

Majlisī, 'Allamah Muḥammad Bāqir, *Biḥār al-Anwār,* Vol. 30, p. 348.

"By God, I will not permit you to drag my cousin away oppressively."[185]

[185] al-Ṭabarī, Muḥammad b. Jarīr, *Nawādir al-Mu'jizāt fī Manāqib al-A'immah al-Hudāt*, p. 183.

Isfahānī, Shaykh 'Abdallah Baḥrānī, *'Awālim al-'Ulūm*, Vol. 11, p. 572.

Qur'ānic View

While it is feasible to understand individuals and entities by contemplating their characteristics and deeds, such understanding is inherently partial and constrained. This is because, firstly, the inner reality of others is only fully known to God ﷻ, and secondly, recognition derived from observation does not fully disclose the truth. Hence, the most effective approach is to gain knowledge through the viewpoint of the Creator ﷻ, who completely understands His creation, including all their innate and developed virtues. Consequently, when seeking to comprehend the essence of Sayyidah Fāṭimah عليها السلام, the optimal method is to refer to the verses of the Noble Qur'ān, which illuminate the hidden truth of Sayyidah Fāṭimah عليها السلام. In this section, we will explore the Qur'ānic view of this esteemed lady.[186]

The Verse of Purification

﴿إِنَّمَا يُرِيدُ اللَّهُ لِيُذْهِبَ عَنكُمُ الرِّجْسَ أَهْلَ الْبَيْتِ وَيُطَهِّرَكُمْ تَطْهِيرًا﴾

﴾'innamā yurīdu llāhu li-yudhhiba ʿankumu r-rijsa 'ahla l-bayti wa-yuṭahhirakum taṭhīra^n﴿

﴾Indeed God desires to repel all impurity from you, O People of the Household, and purify you with a thorough purification﴿[187]

[186] Āmulī, Āyatullāh ʿAbd Allāh Jawādī, *Hamtāyī Qur'ān wa Ahl al-Bayt* عليهم السلام, p. 151-152 and 156-157.

[187] Sūrat al-Aḥzāb, Verse 33.

Despite the debates and disputes from enemies concerning the Verse of Infallibility, no one can deny that the verse was revealed about the Ahl al-Bayt ؑ, namely the Prophet ﷺ, Imām ʿAlī, Sayyidah Fāṭimah, Imām al-Ḥasan and Imām al-Ḥusayn ؑ. The only argument they make is for the inclusion of others. Hence, it is unanimous that this verse is about Sayyidah Fāṭimah ؑ.

This esteemed verse, which is absolute, signifies the virtues of the Prophet ﷺ and the Ahl al-Bayt ؑ being devoid of impurities and purified from any form of error. As corroborated by other authentic narrations, this suggests their freedom from faults, transgressions, and mistakes. Their absolute infallibility extends beyond their divine duties to encompass all personal matters, whether religious, moral, or ethical – they are exempt from these shortcomings.

The prerequisite for absolute infallibility is that this avoidance of impurity and purification of the soul must have been present from the moment of creation, not as a result of progressive purification. It would be illogical to suggest that impurities could approach the Prophet ﷺ only for God ﷻ to eliminate them. Furthermore, the Prophet's ﷺ matter originates from the same root as the Ahl al-Bayt ؑ. If this were not the case, the Noble Qur'ān would have made separate references to them. Therefore, according to the verse, Sayyidah Fāṭimah ؑ, like her

---

[188] Āmulī, Āyatullāh ʿAbd Allāh Jawādī, *Hamtāyī Qur'ān wa Ahl al-Bayt* ؑ, p. 160-161.

The discourse on infallibility and God's ﷻ intention to expel impurity and thoroughly cleanse the Ahl al-Bayt ؏ has led many to boast about their status, attempting to incorporate themselves into the Ahl al-Bayt ؏. The Ahl al-Bayt ؏ frequently cited this verse as evidence of their righteousness, sometimes using it to challenge their adversaries and, at other times, to articulate their stance. For example, when Imām Sajjād (Imām Zayn al-'Ābidīn) ؏ was incarcerated due to Ummayid animosity, and the Syrians labeled him a foreigner, he once defended his righteousness to a Syrian man who sought to belittle him. He referred to the Noble verse, asking:

"Have you read the verse: *"Indeed God desires to repel all impurity from you..."?"*[189]

The man responded:

"Is this verse about you?"

The Imām ؏ affirmed:

"Yes, this verse refers to us."[190]

---

[189] The *Verse of Purification* at the beginning of this chapter.

[190] al-Ṭabarī, Muḥammad, *Jāmi' al-Bayān*, Vol. 22, p. 7.

Ṭabrisī, Shaykh Aḥmad b. 'Alī Ṭabrisī, *al-Iḥtijāj*, Vol. 2, p. 307.

Imām Muḥammad al-Bāqir ﷺ also describes the virtues of his pure lineage and their uniqueness, saying:

> "How can you describe a people from whom God ﷻ removes impurities?"[191]

On the day of the council that resulted in 'Usmān's selection, Amīr al-Mu'minīn ﷺ referred to this verse and questioned:

> "I solemnly swear to God ﷻ, is there anyone among you to whom the Verse of Purification was revealed? When the Prophet took me, Fāṭimah, al-Ḥasan, and al-Ḥusayn under the cloak and prayed:
>
> > 'Oh God, these are my Ahl al-Bayt. Hence, cleanse them of impurities.'"

The council members responded in the negative.[192]

---

[191] Kulaynī, Shaykh Muḥammad b. Ya'qūb, *al-Kāfī,* Vol. 2, p. 182.

al-Ḥuwayzī, al-'Arūsī, *Tafsīr Nūr al-Thaqalayn,* Vol. 4, p. 284.

Āmulī, Āyatullāh 'Abd Allāh Jawādī, *Hamtāyī Qur'ān wa Ahl al-Bayt* ﷺ, p. 157.

[192] Ṣadūq, Shaykh Muḥammad b. 'Alī, *al-Khiṣāl,* Vol. 2, p. 561.

al-Ḥuwayzī, al-'Arūsī, *Tafsīr Nūr al-Thaqalayn,* Vol. 4, p. 282.

Unquestionably, the Holy Prophet ﷺ is counted among the Ahl al-Bayt عليهم السلام, and indeed, he is the authorized interpreter of the revelation:

﴿بِالْبَيِّنَاتِ وَالزُّبُرِ ۗ وَأَنزَلْنَا إِلَيْكَ الذِّكْرَ لِتُبَيِّنَ لِلنَّاسِ مَا نُزِّلَ إِلَيْهِمْ وَلَعَلَّهُمْ يَتَفَكَّرُونَ﴾

﴾*bi-l-bayyināti wa-z-zuburi wa-'anzalnā 'ilayka dh-dhikra li-tubayyina li-n-nāsi mā nuzzila 'ilayhim wa-la'allahum yatafakkarūna*﴿

﴾*[and sent them] with manifest proofs and scriptures. We have sent down the reminder to* you *so that* you *may clarify for the people that which has been sent down to them, so that they may reflect*﴿[193]

Thus, the genuine interpretation and elucidation of the Noble Qur'ān originates from the Holy Prophet ﷺ or is directed towards him. Consequently, the responsibility of interpreting the Verse of Purification rests with him. The

[193] Sūrat an-Naḥl, Verse 44.

Prophet carried out this divine duty in various manners.[194]

Abū Saʿīd Khudrī narrates from the Prophet:

> "The Verse of Purification was revealed for five people: myself, ʿAlī, Fāṭimah, al-Ḥasan, and al-Ḥusayn."[195]

The Verse of Purification was revealed to the Prophet while he was in Umm Salmah's house. The Prophet then called for Imām al-Ḥasan, Imām al-Ḥusayn, Sayyidah

---

[194] Abū Baṣīr narrates from Imām Jaʿfar al-Ṣādiq, who in turn quotes the Prophet:

> "I will leave for you the book of God and my Ahl al-Bayt, as I have requested God to ensure these two never separate until they join me at the pond of Kawthar, a request that God has granted. Do not presume to instruct my Ahl al-Bayt, for their knowledge surpasses yours [in all matters]. My Ahl al-Bayt will not misguide you nor lead you into the abyss of error."

Imām Jaʿfar al-Ṣādiq then added,

> "Had the Messenger of God not explicitly identified the members of the Ahl al-Bayt, certain individuals would have claimed to be part of the Ahl al-Bayt."

Kulaynī, Shaykh Muḥammad b. Yaʿqūb, *al-Kāfi,* Vol. 1, p. 286-287.

al-Ḥuwayzī, al-ʿArūsī, *Tafsīr Nūr al-Thaqalayn,* Vol. 4, p. 274.

[195] al-Suyūṭī, Jalāl al-Dīn, *al-Durr al-Manthūr,* Vol. 5, p. 198.

Fāṭimah, and Imām 'Alī ☾ and gathered them around him. After reciting this verse, he draped his woolen garment over their heads and declared:

"These are my Ahl al-Bayt! Oh God, keep them away from impurities and cleanse them."

Witnessing this, Umm Salmah asked:

"Oh, Messenger of God! Am I also a subject of this verse?"

He ☼ responded:

"You possess your virtues and are on the path of righteousness."[196]

Concerning this matter, the subsequent statements have been attributed to Umm Salmah:

---

[196] The content of this narration has been mentioned by most Shī'ah and Sunnī narrators, for more information refer to:

al-Suyūṭī, Jalāl al-Dīn, al-Durr al-Manthūr, Vol. 5, p. 198-199.

al-Ṭabarī, Muḥammad, Jāmi' al-Bayān, Vol. 22, p. 6-8.

al-Ḥākim al-Ḥaskānī, Shawāhid al-Tanzīl li Qawā'id al-Tafḍīl, Vol. 2, p. 26-139.

a. The Messenger of God ﷺ said to me:

"You embody virtue, and you are among my wives."

However, he never stated:

"You belong to my Ahl al-Bayt."[197]

b. The Prophet ﷺ said to me:

"You are one of my worthy women."

But if he had told me that you are from my Ahl al-Bayt, it would have been better for me than everything the sun shines and sets on."[198]

c. The Prophet ﷺ spread his cloak on the ground and sat everyone on it. Then he took the four sides of the robe and put it over their heads. Then, raising his right hand, he said:

---

[197] al-Ḥākim al-Ḥaskānī, *Shawāhid al-Tanzīl li Qawāʿid al-Tafḍīl,* Vol. 2, p. 124.

Majlisī, ʿAllamah Muḥammad Bāqir, *Biḥār al-Anwār,* Vol. 25, p. 214.

[198] al-Ḥākim al-Ḥaskānī, *Shawāhid al-Tanzīl li Qawāʿid al-Tafḍīl,* Vol. 2, p. 133.

> "This is my Ahl al-Bayt, so repel all impurity from them and purify them with a thorough purification."[199]

The collective interpretation of these narrations underscores how the Prophet ﷺ emphasized the significance of the Verse of Purification while identifying and defining the members of the Ahl al-Bayt عليهم السلام. Undoubtedly, Umm Salmah holds a distinguished position and is considered one of the Prophet's ﷺ esteemed wives. She is greatly revered by both Shī'ah and Sunnī schools of thought, and the infallible Imāms عليهم السلام would respectfully mention her name. However, the Prophet ﷺ did not count her among the members of the Ahl al-Bayt. When she attempted to lift the cloak to join them, the Prophet ﷺ held her back.

It is crucial to note that the event that transpired in Umm Salmah's home is a testament to her elevated status and respect for this distinguished lady. Her being denied entry signals to others that if Umm Salmah, despite all her virtues, was not permitted to join, then it is highly unlikely

---

[199] al-Ṭabarī, Muḥammad, *Jāmi' al-Bayān,* Vol. 22, p. 7.

that others would be considered members of the Ahl al-Bayt ﷺ.[200]

After the revelation of the Verse of Purification, for a long time, the Prophet ﷺ would stand at the door of Sayyidah Fāṭimah al-Zahrā' ﷺ and place his hands on the frame of the door and say:

> "Peace be upon you, Ahl al-Bayt and may God ﷻ send His Mercy and Blessings on you, '*Indeed God desires to repel all impurity from you, O People of the Household, and purify you with a thorough purification...*'[201] I am at peace with those who make peace with you, and I am at war with those who make war with you.

---

[200] This event has been narrated in more detail by Sayyidah Fāṭimah ﷺ and is widely known as Ḥadīth al-Kisā' which has been mentioned in the book *Mafātīḥ al-Jinān*. The comparison of Ḥadīth al-Kisā' with other ḥadīth increases the possibility that this event also took place in the house of Sayyidah Fāṭimah ﷺ.

Shūshtarī, Qāẓī Nūrallāh, *Iḥqāq al-Ḥaqq wa Izhāq al-Bāṭil*, Vol. 2, p. 555.

Isfahānī, Shaykh 'Abdallah Baḥrānī, *'Awālim al-'ulūm*, Vol. 11, p. 931.

[201] Sūrat al-Aḥzāb, Verse 33.

Ibn 'Abbās narrates that the Prophet ﷺ repeated this act five times a day after every prayer.[202]

Various accounts suggest that the Prophet ﷺ maintained this practice for an extended period, with some reports indicating six months and others up to nine months.[203] Many narrations suggest that he continued this until his last days. One such narration from Abū al-Ḥamrā' recounts that the Prophet ﷺ would approach the door every morning after prayer, grasp the frame, and extend his salām, receiving a response from within the house. He would then say,

> "Pursue [your daily] prayers, may God's ﷻ Mercy be upon you. God ﷻ wishes to remove all impurity from you, O People of the Household, and cleanse you with a thorough purification."

Nafī' b. Ḥārith, the narrator of this event, inquired from Abū al-Ḥamrā',

> "Who were the occupants of the house?"

---

[202] al-Suyūṭī, Jalāl al-Dīn, *al-Durr al-Manthūr,* Vol. 5, p. 199.

Āmulī, Āyatullāh 'Abd Allāh Jawādī, *Hamtāyī Qur'ān wa Ahl al-Bayt* ﷺ, p. 170.

[203] al-Ḥākim al-Ḥaskānī, *Shawāhid al-Tanzīl li Qawā'id al-Tafḍīl,* Vol. 2, p. 75-81.

Abū al-Ḥamrā' responded,

> "'Alī, Fāṭimah, al-Ḥasan, and al-Ḥusayn."[204]

Given that this narration does not specify an end of the action, it is reasonable to infer that he continued this practice until his final days, considering that the narration from Sayūṭī citing Ibn 'Abbās is narrated in the same manner.

The narration from Abū al-Ḥamrā' is presented more comprehensively in Shī'ah sources, stating:

> "The Prophet continued in this practice until his final days."[205]

Imām al-Ḥasan al-Mujtabā ﷺ, upon accepting the peace treaty he mentioned in his speech:

> "Until the end of his life, the Prophet ﷺ would come to us for every morning prayer and say:

---

[204] The esteemed Sunnī scholar, Ḥākim Ḥaskānī, has referenced this narration and others of similar context. The time above periods are also cited in the same manner. These narrations are included in the second volume of his book, *Shawāhid al-Tanzīl li Qawā'id al-Tafḍīl.*

Āmulī, Āyatullāh 'Abd Allāh Jawādī, *Hamtāyī Qur'ān wa Ahl al-Bayt* ﷺ, p. 171.

[205] al-Qummī, 'Alī b. Ibrāhīm, *Tafsīr al-Qummī,* Vol. 2, p. 67.

"God's ﷻ peace and blessings be upon you..."[206]

Regardless, this possibility is strongly supported by the fact that Madīnah was a hub of activity where various groups would visit, interact with, and learn from the Prophet ﷺ. They would listen to Qur'ānic verses, acquire knowledge of Islāmic laws, and get their queries answered. It is plausible that the Prophet ﷺ acted in this way to acquaint newcomers with the stature of the Ahl al-Bayt ﵈ and to remind the people of Madīnah about this significant issue continually.

In the Verse of Purification, the term Ahl al-Bayt ﵈ refers to the household of the Prophet ﷺ, and it is linked to al-Nabūwat with a lām (Ahl al-Bayt li-Nabūwat). Thus, the household is associated with the status of prophethood, not specifically with the individual, Muḥammad b. ʿAbdullāh ﷺ, a resident of Makkah or Madīnah. Given the casual interactions and relative dependencies among households, one might attribute this as a reason for association with the mentioned verse. However, this connection alone is insufficient. This household must embody the same qualities and virtues inherent to the position of prophethood. As per the verse's testimony, Sayyidah Fāṭimah ﵛ, her husband ﵇, and their pure children ﵈ were endowed with these perfections, along

---

[206] Ṭūsī, Shaykh Muḥammad b. Ḥasan, *al-Amālī*, p. 565.

Āmulī, Āyatullāh ʿAbd Allāh Jawādī, *Hamtāyī Qur'ān wa Ahl al-Bayt* ﵈, p. 172.

with the religious and moral virtues corresponding with the position of prophethood.[207]

The Verse of Mubāhalah

﴿فَمَنْ حاجَّكَ فيهِ مِن بَعدِ ما جاءَكَ مِنَ العِلمِ فَقُل تَعالَوا نَدعُ أَبناءَنا وَأَبناءَكُم وَنِساءَنا وَنِساءَكُم وَأَنفُسَنا وَأَنفُسَكُم ثُمَّ نَبتَهِل فَنَجعَل لَعنَتَ اللَّهِ عَلَى الكاذِبينَ﴾

﴿fa-man ḥājjaka fīhi min baʿdi mā jāʾaka mina l-ʿilmi fa-qul taʿālaw nadʿu ʾabnāʾanā wa-ʾabnāʾakum wa-nisāʾanā wa-nisāʾakum wa-ʾanfusanā wa-ʾanfusakum thumma nabtahil fa-najʿal laʿnata llāhi ʿalā l-kādhibīna﴾

﴿Should anyone argue with you concerning him, after the knowledge that has come to you, say, 'Come! Let us call our sons and your sons, our women and your women, our souls and your souls, then let us pray earnestly and call down God's curse upon the liars'﴾[208]

The Christians of Najrān, who held the belief that ʿĪsā ﷺ was the son of God, disputed the Prophet's ﷺ claims about the miraculous birth of Prophet ʿĪsā ﷺ without a father.

---

[207] Āmulī, Āyatullāh ʿAbd Allāh Jawādī, *Tajalī Wilāyat dar Āyat Taṭhīr*, p. 54-55.

[208] Sūrat Āl ʿImrān, Verse 61.

After their persistent objections, the Verse of Mubāhalah was revealed. The Prophet ﷺ then declared,

> "Let us lift our hands towards the heavens and implore God ﷻ to triumph over the truth and eradicate falsehood."

Following the meeting, the bishop of Najrān advised his delegates,

> "If you see Muḥammad arrive with his family and children, do not proceed with the Mubāhalah."

This is precisely what transpired. Everyone witnessed that day as the Prophet ﷺ arrived with Sayyidah Fāṭimah and Imām ʿAlī ؑ, and he said:

> "Oh God ﷻ, this is my household."

Then instructed them:

> "When I make the prayer, say 'Āmīn.'"

When the leader of Najrān recognized them, he said to his companions:

> "Oh people, I see faces that, if they were to implore God to topple a mountain, He would oblige. Do not provoke them, or you will face destruction, and no

> Christian will survive on earth until the Day of Judgement."[209]

Both Shīʿah and Sunnī interpreters concur that the term "our souls" in the verse refers to Imām ʿAlī, "our sons" signifies Imām al-Ḥasan and Imām al-Ḥusayn ﷺ, and "our women" denotes solely Sayyidah Fāṭimah ﷺ.[210] It is worth noting that while the verse's invitation extends to all children, women, and souls,[211] The Prophet ﷺ included only these four individuals, which serves as a testament to their preeminence over all other children, women, and souls.

---

[209] ar-Rāzī, Fakhr ad-Dīn, *Mafātīḥ al-Ghayb* (*al-Tafsīr al-Kabīr*), Vol. 8, p. 247.

al-Irdibillī, ʿAlī b. ʿIsā Hakkārī, *Kashf al-Ghummah fī Maʿrifat al-Aʾimma,* Vol. 1, p. 234.

[210] al-Ḥuwayzī, al-ʿArūsī, *Tafsīr Nūr al-Thaqalayn,* Vol. 1, p. 349.

al-Ḥākim al-Ḥaskānī, *Shawāhid al-Tanzīl li Qawāʿid al-Tafḍīl,* Vol. 1, p. 163.

al-Wāhidī, ʿAlī b. Aḥmad, *Asbāb al-Nuzūl,* p. 108.

[211] If the plural of these words (ʾabnāʾ, nisāʾ, ʾanfus) are attached to a pronoun, it signifies all people.

The Verse of Muwaddat (Love)[212]

﴿قُل لا أَسأَلُكُم عَلَيهِ أَجرًا إِلَّا المَوَدَّةَ فِي القُربىٰ ۗ وَمَن يَقتَرِف حَسَنَةً نَزِد لَهُ فيها حُسنًا ۚ إِنَّ اللَّهَ غَفورٌ شَكورٌ﴾

﴿qul lā 'as'alukum 'alayhi 'ajran 'illā l-mawaddata fī l-qurbā wa-man yaqtarif ḥasanatan nazid lahū fīhā ḥusnan 'inna llāha ghafūrun shakūr^un^﴾

﴿Say, *'I do not ask you any reward for it except love of [my] relatives.' Whoever performs a good deed, We shall enhance for him its goodness. Indeed God is Forgiving, Appreciative*﴾[213]

This verse establishes that God ﷻ Himself has made it obligatory for all Muslims to harbor a love for Sayyidah Fāṭimah عليها السلام, who is the nearest kin of the Prophet ﷺ. This signifies Fāṭimah عليها السلام 's special relationship with God ﷻ.

Ibn 'Abbās has said:

> "Since Islām gained strength in Madīnah after the migration, the Anṣār said:

---

[212] Āmulī, Āyatullāh 'Abd Allāh Jawādī, *Adab Finā' al-Muqaribān*, Vol. 2, p. 280.

[213] Sūrat ash-Shūrā, Verse 23.

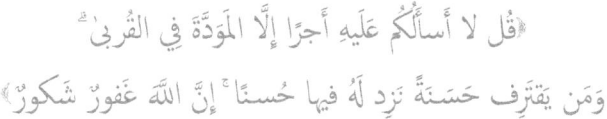

'Let us go to the Prophet ﷺ and tell him that in the troubles that arise, our properties are at his disposal and he can use them [however he likes]."

The noble verse was revealed:

﴾Say, *'I do not ask you any reward for it except love of [my] relatives.' Whoever performs a good deed, We shall enhance for him its goodness. Indeed God is Forgiving, Appreciative*﴿[214] [215]

Ibn ʿArabī states:

"The verse broadly implies the refusal of seeking reward, as the benefits of friendship and love for the Ahl al-Bayt are inherent to their admirers. Love necessitates a spiritual affinity between the admirer and the admired, serving as the basis for their mutual closeness. Thus, one can only be their admirer if they love God ﷻ and His messenger, leading to God ﷻ and His messenger returning their love. If God did not love

---

[214] Ṭabrisī, Shaykh Faḍl b. Ḥasan, *Majmaʿ al-Bayān fī Tafsīr al-Qur'ān,* Vol. 9, p. 44.

Istarābādī, Sharaf al-Dīn Ḥusaynī, *Ta'wīl al-Āyāt al-Ẓāhirah*, p. 531.

Majlisī, ʿAllamah Muḥammad Bāqir, *Biḥār al-Anwār,* Vol. 23, p. 231.

[215] Sūrat ash-Shūrā, Verse 23.

them ﷺ, His messenger would not have loved them either. The Ahl al-Bayt عليهم السلام subjects are these four individuals referenced in the narrations."[216]

Then he mentions Ibn 'Abbās' narration, in which the Messenger of God ﷺ asks,

> "Who are the relatives upon whom love is obligatory for all Muslims?"

He replies,

> "'Alī, Fāṭimah, and her two sons."[217]

'Allāmah Ṭabrisī documents that the Prophet ﷺ stated:

> "God ﷻ crafted the prophets from various trees, but 'Alī and I were formed from the same tree. I am the tree's stem, while 'Alī is its branch, Fāṭimah is its flower, al-Ḥasan and al-Ḥusayn are its fruits, and our followers are the leaves of this tree. Salvation is promised to anyone who touches one of its branches. However, if someone strays from this tree, they will fall, regardless of whether they have worshipped [God ﷻ] for a thousand [years]. If someone grows old like musk but lacks love for us, God ﷻ will cast them into the Fire, starting from their head."

---

[216] Ibn 'Arabī, *Tafsīr Ibn 'Arabī*, Vol. 2, p. 231.

[217] Zamakhsharī, Maḥmūd b. 'Umar, *al-Kashāf*, Vol. 4, p. 219-220.

Following this, the Prophet recited the Verse of Muwaddat.[218]

The Ahl al-Bayt are cherished by God and His Prophet, with Sayyidah Fāṭimah holding a unique status among them. When Amīr al-Mu'minīn inquired from the Prophet:

"Among us, who is more loved? Is it me or Fāṭimah?"

The Prophet responded:

"Fāṭimah is more beloved, and you are dearer."[219]

This could be because both are embodiments of the Kawthar, a divine blessing given to the Prophet, making them both adored and esteemed.

---

[218] Ṭabrisī, Shaykh Faḍl b. Ḥasan, *Majma' al-Bayān fī Tafsīr al-Qur'ān,* Vol. 9, p. 43.

[219] Ibn Shahrāshūb, Muḥammad b. 'Alī, *Manāqib Āl Abī Ṭālib,* Vol. 3, p. 331.

Abū Bakr, Ḥumaydī, *Musnad Ḥumaydī,* Vol. 1, p. 23.

Sūrat al-Kawthar[220]

﴿إِنَّا أَعْطَيْنَاكَ الْكَوْثَرَ﴾

﴿'innā 'a'ṭaynāka l-kawthar﴾

﴿فَصَلِّ لِرَبِّكَ وَانْحَرْ﴾

﴿fa-ṣalli li-rabbika wa-nḥar﴾

﴿إِنَّ شَانِئَكَ هُوَ الْأَبْتَرُ﴾

﴿'innā shāni'aka huwa l-'abtar﴾

﴿*Indeed We have given* you *abundance. So pray to* your *Lord, and sacrifice [the sacrificial camel].* Indeed it is* your *enemy who is without posterity*﴾[221]

When the Prophet experienced the loss of his two children, 'Abdullāh and Qāsim, he was ridiculed by those around him. Individuals like 'Āṣ b. Wā'il even referred to the

---

220 Āmulī, Āyatullāh 'Abd Allāh Jawādī, *Tasnīm fī Tafsīr al-Qur'ān,* Vol. 18, p. 163.

221 Sūrat al-Kawthar, Verse 1-3.

* Or 'raise your hands.' According to this interpretation, the phrase refers to the raising of the hands to the ears during prayers.

Prophet ﷺ as *abtar*, implying he had no lineage.[222] This was a severe and distressing experience for the Prophet ﷺ. However, the Prophet's ﷺ spirits were lifted when God ﷻ revealed this Sūrah.

There are twenty-five interpretations for the term *Kawthar*, the most evident being the existence of Sayyidah Fāṭimah ﷺ. 'Allāmah Ṭabāṭabā'ī ؒ points out that the Prophet's ﷺ enemies would label him as abtar. Given this context, the most reasonable interpretation of the term could be Sayyidah Fāṭimah ﷺ.[223]

Fakhr Rāzī further elaborates:

> "The term *Kawthar* signifies the progeny of the Prophet ﷺ, as the verses counter those who mocked the Prophet ﷺ by stating:
>
> > 'He has no son.'
>
> Thus, the essence of Kawthar is that God ﷻ blessed him with descendants who would endure."[224]

---

222 al-Suyūṭī, Jalāl al-Dīn, *al-Durr al-Manthūr,* Vol. 6, p. 404.

223 Ṭabāṭabā'ī, 'Allamah Sayyid Muḥammad Ḥusayn, *al-Mīzān fī Tafsīr al-Qur'ān,* Vol. 20, p. 370.

224 ar-Rāzī, Fakhr ad-Dīn, *Mafātīḥ al-Ghayb* (*al-Tafsīr al-Kabīr*), Vol. 32, p. 313.

Based on this, the day Sayyidah Fāṭimah ﷤ entered this world, the enemies of the Prophet ﷺ became abtar and hopeless.

Sayyidah Fāṭimah ﷤ was bestowed with the name Kawthar, a great honor given by God ﷻ to His Prophet ﷺ. This not only flourished the lineage and descendants of God's ﷻ most devout servants on earth, but the very existence of this esteemed lady became a fountain of numerous blessings for the world. If it were not for Sayyidah Fāṭimah ﷤, the Holy Prophet's ﷺ endeavors would have been in vain, and the name of Islām would have remained unknown. It was entirely due to her relentless efforts to safeguard the sanctity of God's ﷻ divine guardian and preserve his life amidst the severe onslaughts of the ignorant. She exposed the early signs of treachery within the Muslim nation, introduced the righteous path of Prophet Muḥammad ﷺ, Sayyidah Fāṭimah ﷤, and Imām 'Alī ﷤ to those seeking guidance until the day of Judgement, and fulfilled her duty of presenting evidence before the people.

On the one hand, she nurtured religious leaders and protectors of the delicate boundaries of faith, and on the other, she elucidated the scripture and tradition. She would receive interpretations of numerous divine verses and news, preserving them in the Ṣaḥīfah Fāṭimah. Consequently, blessings would not emanate from any source other than through the divine grace of Fāṭimah ﷤. Indeed, Sayyidah Fāṭimah ﷤ is the very divine gift that God ﷻ bestowed upon His Messenger as a token of his gratitude and sacrifice.

Sūrat al-Qadr[225]

﴿إِنَّا أَنزَلْنَاهُ فِي لَيْلَةِ الْقَدْرِ﴾

﴾'innā 'anzalnāhu fī laylati l-qadrⁱ﴿

﴿وَمَا أَدْرَاكَ مَا لَيْلَةُ الْقَدْرِ﴾

﴾wa-mā 'adrāka mā laylatu l-qadrⁱ﴿

﴿لَيْلَةُ الْقَدْرِ خَيْرٌ مِنْ أَلْفِ شَهْرٍ﴾

﴾laylatu l-qadri khayrun min 'alfi shahrⁱⁿ﴿

﴿تَنَزَّلُ الْمَلَائِكَةُ وَالرُّوحُ فِيهَا بِإِذْنِ رَبِّهِمْ مِنْ كُلِّ أَمْرٍ﴾

﴾tanazzalu l-malā'ikatu wa-r-rūḥu fīhā bi-'idhni rabbihim min kulli 'amrⁱⁿ﴿

---

225 Āmulī, Āyatullāh 'Abd Allāh Jawādī, *Sarūsh Hidāyat,* Vol. 2, p. 155.

Āmulī, Āyatullāh 'Abd Allāh Jawādī, *Imām Mahdī Mawjūd Maw'ūd,* p. 62.

﴿سَلامٌ هِيَ حَتَّىٰ مَطلَعِ الفَجرِ﴾

﴿salāmun hiya ḥattā maṭlaʿi l-fajr﴾

﴿Indeed We sent it down on the Night of Ordainment. What will show you what is the Night of Ordainment? The Night of Ordainment is better than a thousand months. In it the angels and the Spirit descend, by the leave of their Lord, with every command. It is peaceful until the rising of the dawn﴾*[226]

In the interpretation of this verse, Imām Jaʿfar al-Ṣādiq ﷺ states:

> "'Layl' symbolizes Fāṭimah, and 'qadr' represents God ﷻ. Thus, anyone who acknowledges her has comprehended Laylat al-Qadr. Fāṭimah ﷺ was indeed named so because creation was derived from her knowledge. The verse: ﴿*The Night of Ordainment is better than a thousand months*﴾[227] implies that she surpasses a thousand believers in virtue, that she is the mother of the believers, and that she embodies the spirit of sanctity."[228]

---

226 Sūrat al-Qadr, Verses 1-5.

* That is, the Qur'ān. See 44:2-5.

227 Sūrat al-Qadr, Verse 2.

228 Furat b. Ibrāhīm, *Tafsīr Furat,* p. 581-582.

The perfect being serves as a reflection of the Noble Qur'ān and its counterpart, and as per Ḥadīth ath-Thaqalayn, they are inseparable.[229] Thus, the Noble Qur'ān represents God's ﷻ inscribed book, while the perfect being embodies His existential and perceptible book. Just as the revelation of the Noble Qur'ān at a specific time bestows value upon that time and night, the manifestation of the perfect being and his descent from God ﷻ also renders that particular time and place auspicious. Indeed, it is possible that a time and place could gain sanctity and prestige through their emanation from an unseen divine source. However, the source of a time's auspiciousness is undoubtedly rooted in His Wisdom. Similarly, the references to Sayyidah Fāṭimah ﷺ are based on the comparison of the truth of Laylat al-Qadr with the status of the Noble Qur'ān and their interconnectedness.

The teachings from the infallible leaders illuminate the unbreakable bond between the Noble Qur'ān and Ahl al-Bayt ﷺ. Ḥadīth ath-Thaqalayn affirms the inseparability of these two truths and their respective judgments. This unity is also reflected in the realm of understanding, implying that the Imāms utilize the Noble Qur'ān to introduce themselves and employ their manifestation to elucidate the Noble Qur'ān. This is because comprehension of one is impossible without the other. On this occasion, Sayyidah Fāṭimah ﷺ will be presented from

[229] Ṣadūq, Shaykh Muḥammad b. 'Alī, *al-Amālī,* p. 415.

a different perspective as the true embodiment of the Laylat al-Qadr.

Sayyidah Fāṭimah ☀ holds the esteemed role of God's representative, a position earned through her profound understanding and intimate connection with God ☀. This is attributed to the union of all essential attributes of such a divine entity within her. As per the Noble Qur'ān's introduction, Sayyidah Fāṭimah ☀ was an exemplary being, worthy of Jibrā'īl's ☀ divine revelation. A clear testament to this was her receipt of *Muṣḥaf Fāṭimah*, a record of past and future events. Naturally, comprehending the truth of such a perfect and all-encompassing being was no simple task, as stated:

> "...because people have been distanced from acknowledging her wisdom [and insight]."[230]

Hence, we do not anticipate comprehending the reality of this luminous entity. Instead, we are encouraged to gain from her insight and wisdom to the greatest extent humanly feasible and strive to draw closer to her persona.

---

[230] Furat b. Ibrāhīm, *Tafsīr Furat*, p. 581.

Majlisī, 'Allamah Muḥammad Bāqir, *Biḥār al-Anwār*, Vol. 43, p. 65.

Sūrat ad-Dahr (Sūrat al-Insān)

﴿وَيُطْعِمُونَ الطَّعَامَ عَلَىٰ حُبِّهِ مِسْكِينًا وَيَتِيمًا وَأَسِيرًا﴾

﴾wa-yuṭʿimūna ṭ-ṭaʿāma ʿalā ḥubbihī miskīnan wa-yatīman wa-ʾasīran﴿

﴿إِنَّمَا نُطْعِمُكُمْ لِوَجْهِ اللَّهِ لَا نُرِيدُ مِنكُمْ جَزَاءً وَلَا شُكُورًا﴾

﴾ʾinnamā nuṭʿimukum li-wajhi llāhi lā nurīdu minkum jazāʾan wa-lā shukūran﴿

﴾They give food, for the love of Him, to the needy, the orphan and the prisoner, [saying,] 'We feed you only for the sake of God. We do not want any reward from you nor any thanks﴿[231]

Numerous interpreters underscore that this verse was revealed in tribute to Sayyidah Fāṭimah ﷺ, her spouse, and their offspring ﷺ. Jalāl al-Dīn Sayūṭī, below these verses, cites a narration from Ibn ʿAbbās:

"This verse was revealed concerning ʿAlī and Fāṭimah."

Bayḍāwī further elaborates on this account, also quoting from Ibn ʿAbbās, who states:

---

231 Sūrat al-Insān, Verse 8-9.

"al-Ḥasan and al-Ḥusayn fell ill. The Prophet, accompanied by a group of Muslims, visited his kin and suggested to ʿAlī:

'It would be beneficial if you made a vow to heal your children.'

Consequently, ʿAlī, Fāṭimah, and Fiḍḍah vowed to fast for three days, and al-Ḥasan and al-Ḥusayn عليهما السلام recovered. This occurred when there was nothing available for saḥūr or ifṭār (pre and post-fast meals). ʿAlī approached Shamʿūn [a Jew] from Khaybar and borrowed three ṣāʿ [a food measure] of barley. Fāṭimah milled one ṣāʿ of the barley, made dough from it, and baked five loaves of bread, which she set out at the time of ifṭār. Suddenly, a destitute man knocked on their door, pleading. She offered him the bread and drank water. She observed the next day's fast in the same state of hunger. When she intended to break her fast with the second-third of barley, an orphan in need arrived, and prioritizing him, she once again broke her fast with water. This pattern repeated on the third day, with the arrival of a needy captive. Subsequently, the angel Jibrāʾīl عليه السلام appeared, revealed this Sūrah, and addressed the Messenger of God ﷺ:

'Oh Muḥammad! You are blessed to have such a family.'"[232]

---

[232] Bayḍāwī, ʿAbdullāh b. ʿUmar, *Anwār al-Tanzīl wa Asrār al-Taʾwīl*, Vol. 5, p. 270-271.

Verses of Abrār (The Pious)

Imām al-Ḥasan al-Mujtabā ﷺ is quoted as saying:

> "I solemnly swear by God ﷻ that the term abrār, wherever it appears in the book of God ﷻ, refers exclusively to ʿAlī b. Abī Ṭālib, Fāṭimah, myself, and al-Ḥusayn ﷺ. This is because we have upheld righteousness in fulfilling our obligations towards our parents. We have adhered to respecting them, seeking their happiness, and refraining from actions that displease them. Our hearts have been engaged in servitude and virtuous deeds, showing aversion to worldly desires, complying with all of God's ﷻ commands, affirming His Oneness, and testifying to His prophet ﷺ."[233]

In line with this overarching principle from the Imām ﷺ, the Noble Qurʾān has honored the abrār on numerous occasions, and all these instances pertain to the Ahl al-Bayt ﷺ, especially Sayyidah Fāṭimah ﷺ. God ﷻ has repeatedly honored this collective known as the abrār in His esteemed book.

---

[233] Ibn Shahrāshūb, Muḥammad b. ʿAlī, *Manāqib Āl Abī Ṭālib,* Vol. 4, p. 2.

A few examples are cited below:

﴿إِنَّ الْأَبْرَارَ يَشْرَبُونَ مِن كَأْسٍ كَانَ مِزَاجُهَا كَافُورًا﴾

﴿'inna l-'abrāra yashrabūna min ka'sin kāna mizājuhā kāfūra^n﴾

﴿عَيْنًا يَشْرَبُ بِهَا عِبَادُ اللَّهِ يُفَجِّرُونَهَا تَفْجِيرًا﴾

﴿'aynan yashrabu bihā 'ibādu llāhi yufajjirūnahā tafjīra^n﴾

﴿يُوفُونَ بِالنَّذْرِ وَيَخَافُونَ يَوْمًا كَانَ شَرُّهُ مُسْتَطِيرًا﴾

﴿yūfūna bi-n-nadhri wa-yakhāfūna yawman kāna sharruhū mustaṭīra^n﴾

﴿وَيُطْعِمُونَ الطَّعَامَ عَلَىٰ حُبِّهِ مِسْكِينًا وَيَتِيمًا وَأَسِيرًا﴾

﴿wa-yuṭ'imūna ṭ-ṭa'āma 'alā ḥubbihī miskīnan wa-yatīman wa-'asīra^n﴾

﴿*Indeed the pious will drink from a cup seasoned with* Kāfūr*, *a spring where the servants of God drink, which they make to gush forth as they please. They fulfill their vows and* *fear a day whose ill will be widespread. They give food, for the love of Him, to the needy, the orphan and the prisoner*﴿[234]

﴿إِنَّ الْأَبْرَارَ لَفِي نَعِيمٍ﴾

﴿*'inna l-'abrāra la-fī na'īm*[in]﴾

﴿عَلَى الْأَرَائِكِ يَنظُرُونَ﴾

﴿*'alā l-'arā'iki yanẓurūn*[a]﴾

﴿*Indeed the pious shall be amid bliss, observing, [as they recline] on couches*﴾[235]

﴿رَبَّنَا إِنَّنَا سَمِعْنَا مُنَادِيًا يُنَادِي لِلْإِيمَانِ أَنْ آمِنُوا بِرَبِّكُمْ فَآمَنَّا ۚ رَبَّنَا فَاغْفِرْ لَنَا ذُنُوبَنَا وَكَفِّرْ عَنَّا سَيِّئَاتِنَا وَتَوَفَّنَا مَعَ الْأَبْرَارِ﴾

﴿*rabbanā 'innanā sami'nā munādiyan yunādī li-l-'īmāni 'an 'āminū bi-rabbikum fa-'āmannā rabbanā fa-ghfir lanā dhunūbanā wa-kaffir 'annā sayyi'ātinā wa-tawaffanā ma'a l-'abrār*[i]﴾

---

[234] Sūrat al-Insān, Verses 5-8.

* Lit., camphor.

[235] Sūrat al-Muṭaffifīn, Verses 22-23.

﴾Our Lord, we have indeed heard a summoner calling to faith, declaring, "Have faith in your Lord!" So we believed. Our Lord, forgive us our sins and absolve us of our misdeeds, and make us die with the pious﴿[236]

Divine Words

﴿فَتَلَقَّىٰ آدَمُ مِن رَّبِّهِ كَلِمَاتٍ فَتَابَ عَلَيْهِ ۚ إِنَّهُ هُوَ التَّوَّابُ الرَّحِيمُ﴾

﴾fa-talaqqā 'ādamu min rabbihī kalimātin fa-tāba 'alayhi 'innahū huwa t-tawwābu r-raḥīmu﴿

﴾Then Ādam received certain words from his Lord, and He turned to him clemently. Indeed He is the Clement, the Merciful﴿[237]

The phrase "receiving the words" here implies that one actively sought divine knowledge with awareness, eagerness, and a desire to embrace these words for action and obedience. These words can be interpreted as an in-depth study of the same divine names taught to Prophet Ādam ﷺ.

Based on textual evidence, the term *Ādam* is viewed as the object (maf'ūl) of the words *fatalaqqī* and *kalāmāt*, which are deemed its subject (fā'il). This suggests that the

[236] Sūrat Āl 'Imrān, Verse 193.

[237] Sūrat al-Baqarah, Verse 37.

imparted information was a partial or comprehensive depiction of the divine names, signifying that it was not merely words or concepts but actual external realities. The narrations present them as an existential truth of the verses of the Noble Qur'ān, who are the Ahl al-Bayt ﷺ and Sayyidah Fāṭimah ﷺ.[238]

The name of Sayyidah Fāṭimah ﷺ is presented alongside Amīr al-Mu'minīn ﷺ as the embodiment of these words because the light of these two divine counterparts has eclipsed others.[239]

Nafs Muṭma'inah (Tranquil Soul)

A heart that finds contentment in the remembrance of God ﷻ and possesses confidence and stability is bound to reach God ﷻ and a unique place in paradise. These uplifting words captivate a person with the boundless ocean of God's ﷻ Mercy, Kindness, and Grace while reminding the heart of that everlasting abode of joy.

---

[238] Ṣadūq, Shaykh Muḥammad b. ʿAlī, *al-Amālī,* p. 75.

Majlisī, ʿAllamah Muḥammad Bāqir, *Biḥār al-Anwār,* Vol. 11, p. 176.

[239] Āmulī, Āyatullāh ʿAbd Allāh Jawādī, *Zan dar Āynah Jalāl wa Jamāl,* p. 143-144.

Imām Ja'far al-Ṣādiq ‌عليه السلام narrates:

> "Upon the moment of death, the apparitions of the Messenger of God, Amīr al-Mu'minīn, Fāṭimah, al-Ḥasan, al-Ḥusayn, and the virtuous Imāms will manifest before the believers. They will be told that these sacred entities are their allies. The dying person will open their eyes to see. Subsequently, a voice will resonate:
>
> > 'Oh heart that found joy in Muḥammad and his Ahl al-Bayt! Return to your Lord, be content with the guardianship, and be gratified with your rewards. Join the fellowship of my servants [Muḥammad and the Ahl al-Bayt] and enter my paradise. There is nothing more cherished than the soul of a believer departing from the body and joining the caller.'"[240]

Undoubtedly, Sayyidah Fāṭimah al-Zahrā' عليها السلام, also known as Rāḍīyyah and Marḍīyyah, holds stature in the universe such that every believer finds themselves under the encompassing shadow of reverence for this sacred figure until they achieve a state of divine contentment and experience this joy in the presence of the Ahl al-Bayt عليهم السلام.

---

[240] Kulaynī, Shaykh Muḥammad b. Ya'qūb, *al-Kāfī*, Vol. 3, p. 127-128.

Majlisī, 'Allamah Muḥammad Bāqir, *Biḥār al-Anwār*, Vol. 6, p. 196.

The Straight Path

God ﷻ says in Sūrat al-Ḥamd (Sūrat al-Fātiḥah) in the words of the believers who ask God ﷻ to guide them on the straight path:

﴿اهدِنَا الصِّرَاطَ المُستَقِيمَ﴾

﴿ihdinā ṣ-ṣirāṭa l-mustaqīma﴾

﴿Guide us on the straight path﴾[241]

And in continuation, this straight path is explained:

﴿صِرَاطَ الَّذِينَ أَنعَمتَ عَلَيهِم غَيرِ المَغضُوبِ عَلَيهِم وَلَا الضَّالِّينَ﴾

﴿ṣirāṭa lladhīna ʾanʿamta ʿalayhim ghayri l-maghḍūbi ʿalayhim wa-lā ḍ-ḍāllīna﴾

﴿the path of those whom You have blessed﴾*[242]

---

[241] Sūrat al-Fātiḥah, Verse 6.

[242] Sūrat al-Fātiḥah, Verse 7.

* For further Qur'ānic references to 'those whom God has blessed,' see 4:69 and 19:58; see also 5:23, 100; 12:6; 27:19; 28:17; 43:59; 48:2.

Imām Ja'far al-Ṣādiq ﷺ states:

> "The phrase in al-Ḥamd, 'the path of those whom You have blessed,' refers to Muḥammad and his descendants.[243]"[244]

However, it is evident that this verse's reference to the Prophet's family ﷺ does not merely suggest a trait but provides a comprehensive portrayal. Thus, Sayyidah Fāṭimah ﷺ, being a daughter of the Prophet of Islām ﷺ, exemplifies this esteemed verse, with God ﷻ having granted them the gift of guidance. In other words, God ﷻ not only presents them as a model of divine guidance but also directs the prayers of sincere worshippers toward the path illuminated by Sayyidah Fāṭimah's ﷺ guidance.

The Keys to Salvation

﴿وَإِذْ قُلْنَا ادْخُلُوا هَٰذِهِ الْقَرْيَةَ فَكُلُوا مِنْهَا حَيْثُ شِئْتُمْ رَغَدًا وَادْخُلُوا الْبَابَ سُجَّدًا وَقُولُوا حِطَّةٌ نَغْفِرْ لَكُمْ خَطَايَاكُمْ ۚ وَسَنَزِيدُ الْمُحْسِنِينَ﴾

﴿wa-'idh qulnā dkhulū hādhihi l-qaryata fa-kulū minhā ḥaythu shi'tum raghadan wa-dkhulū l-bāba sujjadan

243 Ṣadūq, Shaykh Muḥammad b. 'Alī, *Ma'ānī al-Akhbār,* p. 36.

Majlisī, 'Allamah Muḥammad Bāqir, *Biḥār al-Anwār,* Vol. 24, p. 13.

244 Āmulī, Āyatullāh 'Abd Allāh Jawādī, *Tasnīm fī Tafsīr al-Qur'ān,* Vol. 1, p. 547.

wa-qūlū ḥiṭṭatun naghfir lakum khaṭāyākum wa-sa-nazīdu l-muḥsinīnᵃ﴿

﴿فَبَدَّلَ الَّذِينَ ظَلَمُوا قَوْلًا غَيْرَ الَّذِي قِيلَ لَهُمْ فَأَنزَلْنَا عَلَى الَّذِينَ ظَلَمُوا رِجْزًا مِّنَ السَّمَاءِ بِمَا كَانُوا يَفْسُقُونَ﴾

﴾fa-baddala lladhīna ẓalamū qawlan ghayra lladhī qīla lahum fa-'anzalnā 'alā lladhīna ẓalamū rijzan mina s-samā'i bi-mā kānū yafsuqūnᵃ﴿

﴾And when We said, 'Enter this town, and eat thereof freely whencesoever you wish, and enter prostrating at the gate, and say, "Relieve [us of the burden of our sins]," ** that We may forgive your iniquities, and soon We will enhance the virtuous.' But the wrongdoers changed the saying with other than what they were told. So We sent down on those who were wrongdoers a plague from the sky because of the transgressions they used to commit﴿*[245]

These two verses serve as a reminder of the tenth divine blessing bestowed upon the children of Isrā'īl by God ﷻ

---

[245] Sūrat al-Baqarah, Verses 58-59.

* This city, according to tradition (see Tafsīr al-Imām al-'Askarī ﷺ), was Arīḥā' or Jericho (or Jerusalem, according to some commentators), an ancient city of Palestine near the northwest shore of the Dead Sea. A stronghold commanding the valley of the lower Jordan River, it was captured and destroyed by Yūsha' (Joshua) forty years later.

** Or '[We beseech] forgiveness [for our sins].'

while listening to their complaints and ingratitude. This blessing marked the end of their forty-year-long wandering in the desert, allowing them to enter a land they had been prohibited from for four decades.[246] Their ingratitude was transformed into God's ﷻ command, bringing an end to the Isrā'īlites' period of wandering in the scorching Sīnā' (Sinai) Desert and leading them into the comfort of the city. This city, part of the holy land, is distinguished by its abundance of divine blessings, as well as its sanctity and honor. The children of Isrā'īl were expected to enter with humility, expressing gratitude for God's ﷻ Blessings, particularly the special entrance of the dome and the place designated for worship.

By uttering the word *ḥiṭṭah*, the Banī Isrā'īl were instructed to cleanse their hearts and souls from the taint of sins through genuine repentance.

As per the narrations, it seems from the verse's wording that they were instructed by God ﷻ to pronounce the word

---

[246] Sūrat al-Mā'idah, Verse 26:

﴿قَالَ فَإِنَّهَا مُحَرَّمَةٌ عَلَيْهِمْ ۛ أَرْبَعِينَ سَنَةً ۛ يَتِيهُونَ فِي الْأَرْضِ ۚ فَلَا تَأْسَ عَلَى الْقَوْمِ الْفَاسِقِينَ﴾

﴾*qāla fa-'innahā muḥarramatun 'alayhim 'arba'īna sanatan yatīhūna fī l-'arḍi fa-lā ta'sa 'alā l-qawmi l-fāsiqīna*﴿

﴾He said, 'It shall be forbidden them for forty years: they shall wander about in the earth. So do not grieve for the transgressing lot.'﴿

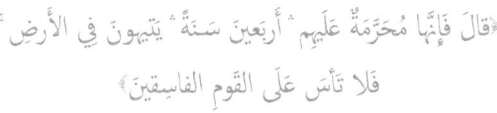

ḥiṭṭah upon entering this door. While the utterance of this specific word signifies a confession of sin and necessitates a spirit of devotion and heartfelt humility, considering the languages spoken, namely Hebrew and Syriac, there is also a possibility that the verse's intent is not merely the pronunciation of the word, but rather to convey an apology and a plea for forgiveness.

In any case, there are some reports, such as the narration quoted from the commentary attributed to Imām Ḥasan al-ʿAskarī ﷺ, and the narration[247] from the Prophet ﷺ concerning part of the verse above.[248] These narrations further corroborate that instead of the word ḥiṭṭah, they uttered another word with similar meaning.[249] The word ḥiṭṭah itself was God's ﷻ will, the utterance of which symbolizes guilt and confession and is not an easy task for the arrogant and defiant. It is worth noting that numerous

---

[247] Via. Sunnī sources.

[248] Sūrat al-Baqarah, Verse 59:

﴿فَبَدَّلَ الَّذِينَ ظَلَمُوا قَوْلًا غَيْرَ الَّذِي قِيلَ لَهُمْ﴾

﴾fa-baddala lladhīna ẓalamū qawlan ghayra lladhī qīla lahum﴿

﴾But the wrongdoers changed the saying with other than what they were told﴿

[249] Imām ʿAskarī, Ḥasan b. ʿAlī, *Tafsīr al-Mansūb ilā Imām al-ʿAskarī*, p. 260.

Ibn Ḥanbal, Aḥmad, *Musnad Aḥmad b. Ḥanbal*, Vol. 2, p. 312.

instances exist where uttering words becomes mandatory, such as in ṣalāh or responding to salām. However, these utterances would only necessitate humility and humiliation if they signify God's ﷻ Greatness or the servitude and obedience of the servant, such as saying *Subḥāna rabbī al-a'lā wa biḥamdih* (Glory be to my Lord, the High, and praise be to Him) during prostration.

As a result, the Isrā'īlī were obliged to do three things in order to be forgiven for their sins:

1. Accessing the city through a specific door, which, as per certain narrations, was low and necessitated stooping to enter.[250] Such an entrance demands one to relinquish pride, humbling even the most arrogant individual. It is worth noting that the act of prostration in this context does not imply bowing, as bending was a prerequisite for entering through this short door.

2. [Have an intention of] I am entering a state of prostration.

3. She was uttering the word ḥiṭṭah while entering.

---

[250] al-Qurṭubī, Muḥammad b. Aḥmad, *Tafsīr al-Qurṭubī: al-Jāmi' Li Aḥkām al-Qur'ān*, Vol. 1, p. 411.

Āmulī, Āyatullāh 'Abd Allāh Jawādī, *Tasnīm fī Tafsīr al-Qur'ān*, Vol. 4, p. 565.

The attraction of prestige led the Banī Isrāʾīl to modify some of these conditions to suit their preferences. At the same time, they readily accepted the command: *eat thereof freely*[251] as it aligned with their desires and cravings. However, they rejected the three commands to such an extent that they openly disputed with Prophet Mūṣā (Moses) ﷺ about the principle of entering the city in a humble and demeaned manner. They rebelled and entered with a defiant and arrogant demeanor. As for the promise of ḥiṭṭah and seeking forgiveness, which, according to some narrations, necessitated them to pronounce the word of tawḥīd and accept the guardianship of the Prophet of Islām ﷺ and the Ahl al-Bayt ﷺ, they arrogantly refused.[252]

When contrasting the Verse of Wilāyah about the Prophet ﷺ and his Ahl al-Bayt ﷺ, we can cite numerous narrations. A few of these are presented here as illustrations:

1. About the two verses:

﴿وَلَيْسَ الْبِرُّ بِأَنْ تَأْتُوا الْبُيُوتَ مِنْ ظُهُورِهَا﴾

﴿*wa-laysa l-birru bi-ʾan taʾtū l-buyūta min ẓuhūrihā*﴾

---

[251] Sūrat al-Baqarah, Verse 58.

[252] Āmulī, Āyatullāh ʿAbd Allāh Jawādī, *Tasnīm fī Tafsīr al-Qurʾān*, Vol. 4, p. 579.

﴾*It is not piety that you come into houses from their rear*﴿[253]

and

﴾وَإِذْ قُلْنَا ادْخُلُوا هَٰذِهِ الْقَرْيَةَ﴿

﴾*wa-'idh qulnā dkhulū hādhihi l-qaryata*﴿

﴾*And when We said, 'Enter this town'*﴿[254]

It has been narrated that Imām 'Alī ﵇ and Imām Muḥammad al-Bāqir ﵇ stated:

"We are those houses which God ﷻ has instructed to be entered through their doors."[255]

---

253 Sūrat al-Baqarah, Verse 189.

254 Sūrat al-Baqarah, Verse 58.

255 Ibn Shahrāshūb, Muḥammad b. 'Alī, *Manāqib Āl Abī Ṭālib*, Vol. 2, p. 34.

Majlisī, 'Allamah Muḥammad Bāqir, *Biḥār al-Anwār*, Vol. 40, p. 205.

2. **Imām Muḥammad al-Bāqir ﷺ has said:**

"We are your door of ḥiṭṭah."[256]

3. **The Prophet ﷺ has said:**

"God ﷻ has placed my family in my nation [Ummah] just like Nūḥ's ark, and the ḥiṭṭah door of Banī Isrā'īl, whoever enters it will be safe."[257]

4. **Imām Muḥammad al-Bāqir ﷺ has said:**

"Jibrā'īl revealed the verse in the following manner:

> "Those who were unjust towards the rights of Muḥammad's family among you altered the words they were instructed to utter. Consequently, We inflicted upon the ones unjust towards the rights of Muḥammad's family a heavenly punishment for their wicked actions."""[258]

---

[256] al-'Ayyāshī, Muḥammad b. Mas'ūd, *Tafsīr al-'Ayyāshī,* Vol. 1, p. 45.

Majlisī, 'Allamah Muḥammad Bāqir, *Biḥār al-Anwār,* Vol. 23, p. 122.

[257] Ṭabrisī, Shaykh Faḍl b. Ḥasan, *Makārim al-Akhlāq,* p. 459.

Majlisī, 'Allamah Muḥammad Bāqir, *Biḥār al-Anwār,* Vol. 74, p. 75.

[258] Kulaynī, Shaykh Muḥammad b. Ya'qūb, *al-Kāfī,* Vol. 1, p. 423-424.

Drawing a comparison between the concept of wilāyah in Islām and the subject of ḥiṭṭah of Banī Isrāʾīl is unproblematic. The most significant insight taken from these narrations is that the authority of the Ahl al-Bayt — particularly Sayyidah Fāṭimah — has been analogized to the salvation of Banī Isrāʾīl. Moreover, numerous narrations about previous prophets and nations suggest that a perfect being like Sayyidah Fāṭimah embodies the true words of God that were spoken by Prophet Ādam and taught to other prophets. At the door of ḥiṭṭah, Banī Isrāʾīl also demonstrated a reverence for this profound truth.[259]

Applying this verse for the Ahl al-Bayt has also appeared in many Sunnī narrations. According to one such narration, the Prophet has said:

"The analogy of my Ahl al-Bayt amongst you is like the door of ḥiṭṭah amongst the Banī Isrāʾīl. Whoever enters that gate will be forgiven."[260] This implies that just as seeking forgiveness leads to the absolution of sins and purification of an individual, turning to the Ahl al-Bayt of the Prophet, particularly its central figure – Sayyidah Fāṭimah al-Zahrāʾ, also results in salvation from impurities.

---

[259] Āmulī, Āyatullāh ʿAbd Allāh Jawādī, *Tasnīm fī Tafsīr al-Qurʾān*, Vol. 4, p. 586.

[260] ʿAlī al-Haythamī, *Majmaʿ al-Zawāʾid*, Vol. 9, p. 168.

God's ﷻ Proof and the Condition of True Faith

﴿آمَنَ الرَّسولُ بِما أُنزِلَ إِلَيهِ مِن رَبِّهِ وَالمُؤمِنونَ ۚ كُلٌّ آمَنَ بِاللَّهِ وَمَلائِكَتِهِ وَكُتُبِهِ وَرُسُلِهِ﴾

﴾'āmana r-rasūlu bi-mā 'unzila 'ilayhi min rabbihī wa-l-mu'minūna kullun 'āmana bi-llāhi wa-malā'ikatihī wa-kutubihī wa-rusulihī﴿

﴾The Apostle has faith in what has been sent down to him from his Lord, and all the faithful. Each [of them] has faith in God, His angels, His scriptures and His apostles﴿[261]

Numerous traditions equate the acknowledgment of Imām 'Alī b. Abī Ṭālib's ؏ guardianship and the infallible Ahl al-Bayt ؏ with belief in God ﷻ, angels, divine scriptures, and prophets. They regard those who affirm the wilāyah of the Ahl al-Bayt ؏ and recognize their esteemed position as true believers. For instance:

1. Abū Salmā, the Prophet's shepherd, recounted that he heard the Messenger of God uttering,

   "On the night of my heavenly ascension, I heard [God say],

[261] Sūrat al-Baqarah, Verse 285.

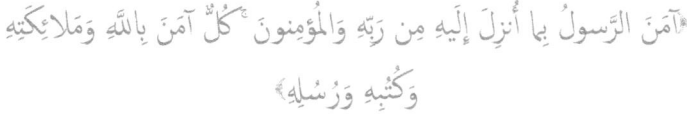

﴾*The Apostle has faith in what has been sent down to him from his Lord*﴿[262]

I [the Prophet ﷺ] said,

'And the believers all believe in God.'

He [God ﷻ] said:

'You have spoken the truth, O Muḥammad. Who will you leave behind as a successor for your nation?'

I [the Prophet ﷺ] replied,

'The most virtuous among them.'

God ﷻ asked,

''Alī b. Abī Ṭālib?'

I [the Prophet ﷺ] confirmed,

'Yes, O Lord.'

God ﷻ declared,

'I present your guardianship to all beings in the heavens and the earth. Whoever accepts it is a

[262] Sūrat al-Baqarah, Verse 285.

believer in my eyes, and whoever denies it is a disbeliever.'

God ﷻ further stated,

'O Muḥammad, if a servant worships Me to the point of being worn out and resembling charred wood, but denies your guardianship, I will not forgive him until he acknowledges your guardianship.'"[263]

2. **Narrated from ʿAbd al-Ṣamad b. Bushayr says:**

I heard from Abā ʿAbdillah (Imām al-Ḥusayn) ﷺ, who said:

"Jibrāʾīl came to the Messenger of God and said God ﷻ says:

﴿آمَنَ الرَّسُولُ بِمَا أُنزِلَ إِلَيْهِ مِن رَّبِّهِ﴾

﴿*ʾāmana r-rasūlu bi-mā ʾunzila ʾilayhi min rabbihī*﴾

[263] Ṭūsī, Shaykh Muḥammad b. Ḥasan, *al-Ghaybah,* p. 147-148.

Majlisī, ʿAllamah Muḥammad Bāqir, *Biḥār al-Anwār,* Vol. 36, p. 262.

﴾*The Apostle has faith in what has been sent down to him from his Lord*﴿[264]

Prophet Muḥammad ﷺ said:

'Yes, my Lord!'

﴿وَالْمُؤْمِنُونَ ۚ كُلٌّ آمَنَ بِاللَّهِ وَمَلَائِكَتِهِ وَكُتُبِهِ وَرُسُلِهِ﴾

﴾*wa-l-mu'minūna kullun 'āmana bi-llāhi wa-malā'ikatihī wa-kutubihī wa-rusulihī*﴿

﴾*and all the faithful. Each [of them] has faith in God, His angels, His scriptures and His apostles*﴿[265]

[Then] God ﷻ said:

﴿لَا يُكَلِّفُ اللَّهُ نَفْسًا إِلَّا وُسْعَهَا﴾

﴾*lā yukallifu llāhu nafsan 'illā wus'ahā*﴿

﴾*God does not task any soul beyond its capacity*﴿[266]

---

[264] Sūrat al-Baqarah, Verse 285.

[265] Sūrat al-Baqarah, Verse 285.

[266] Sūrat al-Baqarah, Verse 286.

Prophet Muḥammad ﷺ says:

﴿رَبَّنَا لَا تُؤَاخِذْنَا﴾

﴿rabbanā lā tu'ākhidhnā﴾

﴿Our Lord! Take us not to task﴾[267]

God ﷻ asked:

> 'O Muḥammad, who is your successor among your people after you?'

Prophet Muḥammad ﷺ said:

> 'God knows best.'

God ﷻ said:

> "Alī, the commander of the faithful.'

Abū 'Abdillāh ﷺ said:

> 'By God, his ['Alī's] guardianship was only given by God directly to Muḥammad.'"[268]

---

[267] Sūrat al-Baqarah, Verse 286.

[268] al-'Ayyāshī, Muḥammad b. Mas'ūd, *Tafsīr al-'Ayyāshī*, Vol. 1, p. 159-160.

3. The Prophet ﷺ says:

> "... O people, say what I have said to you, and salute 'Alī as the leader of the believers, and say:
>
> > 'We hear and obey. Our Lord, forgive us, and toward You is the return.'"[269]

In Sunnī sources, there are similar references under this noble verse. For instance, a narration from the Prophet's ﷺ sheppard narrated that when the Prophet ﷺ ascended to heaven, God ﷻ said to him:

> ﴾*The Apostle has faith in what has been sent down to him from his Lord, and all the faithful*﴿[270]

The Prophet ﷺ says:

> 'The faithful?'

God ﷻ replies:

> 'You have spoken the truth. Who will you leave behind as your successor?'

---

[269] Ṭabrisī, Shaykh Aḥmad b. 'Alī Ṭabrisī, *al-Iḥtijāj,* Vol. 1, p. 66.

Majlisī, 'Allamah Muḥammad Bāqir, *Biḥār al-Anwār,* Vol. 37, p. 217.

[270] Sūrat al-Baqarah, Verse 285.

The Prophet ﷺ said:

'The best of them.'

God ﷻ asked:

''Alī b. Abī Ṭālib?'

The Prophet ﷺ replied affirmatively.

God ﷻ then said:

'O Muḥammad! I created you, 'Alī, al-Ḥasan, al-Ḥusayn, and the children of al-Ḥusayn all from one light. I presented your guardianship to all the heavens and earth beings. O Muḥammad! If a servant worships Me to the point of being worn out and resembling charred wood but denies your guardianship, I will not forgive him until he acknowledges your guardianship.'

Then He ﷻ asked,

'O Muḥammad! Would you like to see your children?'

The Prophet ﷺ replied,

'Yes.'

God ﷻ said,

'Look to the right side of the Throne.'

When the Prophet ﷺ looked, he saw Imām ʿAlī, Sayyidah Fāṭimah, Imām al-Ḥasan, Imām al-Ḥusayn, Imām ʿAlī b. al-Ḥusayn, Imām Muḥammad b. ʿAlī, Imām Jaʿfar b. Muḥammad, Imām Mūsā b. Jaʿfar, Imām ʿAlī b. Mūsā, Imām Muḥammad b. ʿAlī, Imām ʿAlī b. Muḥammad, Imām Ḥasan b. ʿAlī ؑ stood in a halo of light emanating from Imām Muḥammad al-Mahdī ؏, who was praying, shining like a bright star.'

God ﷻ said:

> 'O Muḥammad! These are my proofs...'"[271]

In the narration mentioned above, the name of Sayyidah Fāṭimah ؑ is mentioned alongside the names of the other members of the Ahl al-Bayt ؑ as proofs of God ﷻ.

The Guide and Leader of people

﴿وَكَيْفَ تَكْفُرُونَ وَأَنتُمْ تُتْلَىٰ عَلَيْكُمْ آيَاتُ اللَّهِ وَفِيكُمْ رَسُولُهُ ۗ وَمَن يَعْتَصِم بِاللَّهِ فَقَدْ هُدِيَ إِلَىٰ صِرَاطٍ مُّسْتَقِيمٍ﴾

[271] al-Khawārazmī, *Maqtal al-Ḥusayn,* Vol. 1, p. 95.

Qundūzī, Sulaymān b. Ibrāhīm, *Yanābīʿ al-Mawaddah lī-Dhawī l-Qūrbā,* Vol. 3, p. 380-381.

Qummī, Ibn Shādhān, *Māʾat al-Manqabat,* p. 38-39.

﴾wa-kayfa takfurūna wa-ʾantum tutlā ʿalaykum ʾāyātu llāhi wa-fīkum rasūluhū wa-man yaʿtaṣim bi-llāhi fa-qad hudiya ʾilā ṣirāṭin mustaqīm^in^﴿

﴾And how would you be faithless while the signs of God are recited to you and His Apostle is in your midst? And whoever takes recourse in God is certainly guided to a straight path﴿[272]

In this verse, God ﷻ challenges the believers: how can you disbelieve when all the elements of faith are laid out before you? The recitation of divine verses should increase your faith. Moreover, the messenger of God ﷺ, who interprets and elucidates these divine verses, is a commendable role model for you. Muslims are directed to shield themselves from adversaries' attraction, seek guidance toward the righteous path, strive for God's ﷻ Grace, and adhere to His pure essence and the verses of the Noble Qurʾān. They are encouraged to emulate the Prophet's actions in their lives. Trusting in God ﷻ and seeking His assistance is the safeguard against all temptations and ideological and moral deviation. Adhering to the example set by the Prophet of Islām ﷺ ensures a correct comprehension and recognition of the divine path.

In the above verse, *rasūl* (apostle) signifies the legislative power of the Prophet ﷺ. It refers to his flawless traditions, and given that all members of the pure Ahl al-Bayt ﷺ

[272] Sūrat Āl ʿImrān, Verse 101.

originate from a single light, it can be inferred that the infallible tradition here pertains to the traditions of these pure personalities. A Qur'ānic analysis allows us to deduce the full content of the thaqalyn narration from this verse alone.[273]

About this verse, a narration from the Prophet ﷺ declares:

> "God ﷻ has designated ʿAlī, his wife, and their offspring عليهم السلام as His ﷻ proofs for all His creation. They are the gateways of knowledge among my people, and anyone who follows them is led to the straight path."[274]

This narration presents Sayyidah Fāṭimah عليها السلام and all the Imāms as God's proofs, guides, and leaders for humanity. Indeed, the essence of this narration is that adhering to the Imāms عليهم السلام and Sayyidah Fāṭimah al-Zahrā' عليها السلام is equivalent to adhering to God ﷻ. In Ziyārat al-Jāmiʿah al-Kabīrah, handed down from Imām ʿAlī al-Hādī عليه السلام, it is said that seeking refuge and appealing to the divine Imāms is essentially seeking the shelter and protection of God ﷻ.[275]

---

[273] Āmulī, Āyatullāh ʿAbd Allāh Jawādī, *Tasnīm fī Tafsīr al-Qur'ān*, Vol. 15, p. 187-190.

[274] al-Ḥākim al-Ḥaskānī, *Shawāhid al-Tanzīl li Qawāʿid al-Tafḍīl*, Vol. 1, p. 76.

Qundūzī, Sulaymān b. Ibrāhīm, *Yanābīʿ al-Mawaddah lī-Dhawī l-Qūrbā*, Vol. 1, p. 197.

[275] Ṣadūq, Shaykh Muḥammad b. ʿAlī, *Man Lā Yaḥḍuruh al-Faqīh*, Vol. 2, p. 613.

Clinging to God ﷻ is to obey the commands, words, and actions of the Ahl al-Bayt ﷺ and Sayyidah Fāṭimah ﷺ.

God's ﷻ Rope

﴿وَاعتَصِموا بِحَبلِ اللَّهِ جَميعًا وَلا تَفَرَّقوا ۚ وَاذكُروا نِعمَتَ اللَّهِ عَلَيكُم إِذ كُنتُم أَعداءً فَأَلَّفَ بَينَ قُلوبِكُم فَأَصبَحتُم بِنِعمَتِهِ إِخوانًا وَكُنتُم عَلىٰ شَفا حُفرَةٍ مِنَ النّارِ فَأَنقَذَكُم مِنها ۗ كَذٰلِكَ يُبَيِّنُ اللَّهُ لَكُم آياتِهِ لَعَلَّكُم تَهتَدونَ﴾

﴿wa-ʿtaṣimū bi-ḥabli llāhi jamīʿan wa-lā tafarraqū wa-dhkurū niʿmata llāhi ʿalaykum ʾidh kuntum ʾaʿdāʾan fa-ʾallafa bayna qulūbikum fa-ʾaṣbaḥtum bi-niʿmatihī ʾikhwānan wa-kuntum ʿalā shafā ḥufratin mina n-nāri fa-ʾanqadhakum minhā ka-dhālika yubayyinu llāhu lakum ʾāyātihī laʿallakum tahtadūn[a]﴾

﴿Hold fast, all together, to God's cord, and do not be divided [into sects]. And remember God's blessing upon you when you were enemies, then He brought your hearts together, so you became brothers with His blessing. And you were on the brink of a pit of Fire, whereat He saved you from it. Thus does God clarify His signs for you so that you may be guided﴾[276]

The path to God ﷻ is an upward climb, necessitating a tool for progress. In this spiritual ascent, humans need a rope, and to avoid straying or falling into pitfalls, they must hold fast to the divine rope. The term *ḥabl* (cord or rope) used

---

[276] Sūrat Āl ʿImrān, Verse 103.

here signifies a long, unbroken object that serves as a means to reach a goal or to secure something. Ḥabl has both a physical and spiritual dimension.[277]

In previous verses, God ﷻ mentions the necessity of clinging to the Lord:

﴿وَمَن يَعتَصِم بِاللَّهِ فَقَد هُدِيَ إِلَىٰ صِراطٍ مُستَقيمٍ﴾

﴿*wa-man ya'taṣim bi-llāhi fa-qad hudiya 'ilā ṣirāṭin mustaqīm*[in]﴾

﴿*And whoever takes recourse in God is certainly guided to a straight path*﴾[278]

In the discussion verse, the word used is *jamī'an* (meaning 'all together'). This shows that the command *'i'taṣimū* (meaning 'hold fast') is not directed to individuals but a collective and societal duty.[279]

---

277 Muṣṭafawī, Mīrzā Hasan, *al-Taḥqīq fī Kalamāt al-Qur'ān al-Karīm*, Vol. 2, p. 161.

Āmulī, Āyatullāh 'Abd Allāh Jawādī, *Tasnīm fī Tafsīr al-Qur'ān*, Vol. 15, p. 216-218.

278 Sūrat Āl 'Imrān, Verse 101.

279 Āmulī, Āyatullāh 'Abd Allāh Jawādī, *Tasnīm fī Tafsīr al-Qur'ān*, Vol. 15, p. 220.

Holding fast to God's ﷻ rope provides the way for a collective ascent. The Prophet ﷺ, who can single-handedly travel up,

﴿فَكَانَ قابَ قَوسَينِ أَو أَدنىٰ﴾

﴿*fa-kāna qāba qawsayni ʾaw ʾadnā*﴾

﴿*until he was within two bows' length or even nearer*﴾[280]

becomes duty-bound to assist his nation in reaching this station:

﴿وَاخفِض جَناحَكَ لِمَنِ اتَّبَعَكَ مِنَ المُؤمِنينَ﴾

﴿*wa-khfiḍ janāḥaka li-mani ttabaʿaka mina l-muʾminīna*﴾

﴿*and lower* your *wing to the faithful who follow* you﴾[281]

Once this happens, it would allow others to spread their wings and take this journey towards God ﷻ. So this path is an ascension, which requires a medium:

﴿يا أَيُّهَا الَّذينَ آمَنُوا اتَّقُوا اللَّهَ وَابتَغوا إِلَيهِ الوَسيلَةَ
وَجاهِدوا في سَبيلِهِ لَعَلَّكُم تُفلِحونَ﴾

---

[280] Sūrat an-Najm, Verse 9.

[281] Sūrat ash-Shūrā, Verse 215.

﴿yā-'ayyuhā lladhīna 'āmanū ttaqū llāha wa-btaghū 'ilayhi l-wasīlata wa-jāhidū fī sabīlihī la'allakum tufliḥūn[a]*﴾*

﴿O you who have faith! Be wary of God, and seek the means of recourse to Him, and wage jihād in His way, so that you may be felicitous﴾[282]

This means the Noble Qur'ān and the Ahl al-Bayt عليهم السلام, which is the complete religion sometimes referred to as *ḥabl al-Matīn*. Some commentators of the Noble Qur'ān upon careful studying of the verses and narrations, have concluded that the rope of God عزّ وجلّ is the Ahl al-Bayt عليهم السلام and the Noble Qur'ān in unison. Imām Muḥammad al-Bāqir عليه السلام says:

"We, the Ahl al-Bayt عليهم السلام, are the rope of God عزّ وجلّ."[283]

---

[282] Sūrat al-Mā'idah, Verse 35.

[283] Ṭabrisī, Shaykh Faḍl b. Ḥasan, *Majma' al-Bayān fī Tafsīr al-Qur'ān,* Vol. 2, p. 805.

In a narration from Sunnī sources, we find a similar statement by Imām Jaʿfar al-Ṣādiq 🌼:

"We are that rope of God 🕌, that He ordered everyone to hold onto and not separate from."[284]

As previously stated, Sayyidah Fāṭimah 🌼 is at the heart of the Ahl al-Bayt 🌼. She is both the ideal model and a divine proof for the infallible Imāms 🌼. This is why the Prophet 🕌 made her contentment and displeasure a measure of God's 🕌 contentment and displeasure. The Prophet 🕌 proclaimed:

"Fāṭimah is the blood of my heart, her children are the fruits of my heart, her husband ʿAlī is the light of my eyes, and his children from Fāṭimah are the trustees of God 🕌. They are the strong rope between Him 🕌 and the people. Whoever grabs this rope will be saved, and whoever rejects it will be his downfall."[285]

---

[284] Ḥaḍramī, Abū Bakr, *Rashfat al-Ṣādī*, p. 70.

al-Shāfiʿī, Muʾmin b. al-Ḥasan al-Shablanjī, *Nūr al-Abṣār fī Manāqib Āl Bayt an-Nabī al-Mukhtār*, p. 1.

al-Ṣabān, Muḥammad ʿAlī, *Isʿāf al-Rāghabīn*, p. 109.

[285] Daylamī, Ḥasan b. Muḥammad, *Irshād al-Qulūb*, Vol. 2, p. 423.

Majlisī, ʿAllamah Muḥammad Bāqir, *Biḥār al-Anwār*, Vol. 23, p. 110.

Her Scientific and Epistemological Life[286]

Sayyidah Fāṭimah ﷺ held a unique position that allowed her to gain Islāmic knowledge directly from her esteemed father. He and his children only truly understood the pure divine teachings, which are self-evident regarding the Prophet's knowledge. Sayyidah Fāṭimah al-Zahrā' ﷺ has been quoted in many narrations from the Prophet ﷺ in various fields such as morality, society, and religion. These include respect for one's wife, neighbor's rights, the virtues of Imām 'Alī ﷺ and his Shī'ah, numerous prophecies, and many supplications. Unfortunately, the Muslim nation did not fully utilize this treasure trove of knowledge. Instead of benefiting from her valuable insights into women's society, the ideal lifestyle, and lessons, they caused her heartache with their betrayal.

Clarification of Divine Teachings

This young woman imparted her wisdom and knowledge to the world at eighteen. Her insights illuminated the interpretation of divine teachings, mirroring the wisdom of her counterpart, Amīr al-Mu'minīn ﷺ.

For devout and unblemished servants such as Sayyidah Fāṭimah ﷺ, a distinct stature exists that is unattainable by others. In such a manner, the whispers and trickeries of Shayṭān do not affect her:

---

286 Āmulī, Āyatullāh 'Abd Allāh Jawādī, *Sarchishmah Andīshah,* Vol. 2, p. 86-98.

﴿وَلَأُغْوِيَنَّهُمْ أَجْمَعِينَ﴾

﴿*wa-la-'ughwiyannahum 'ajma'īn*[a]﴾

﴿إِلَّا عِبَادَكَ مِنْهُمُ الْمُخْلَصِينَ﴾

﴿*'illā 'ibādaka minhumu l-mukhlaṣīn*[a]﴾

﴿*and I will surely pervert them, all except Your exclusive servants among them*﴾[287]

Individuals like these do not perpetually doubt their decisions:

﴿فَكَذَّبُوهُ فَإِنَّهُمْ لَمُحْضَرُونَ﴾

﴿*fa-kadhdhabūhu fa-'innahum la-muḥḍarūn*[a]﴾

﴿إِلَّا عِبَادَ اللَّهِ الْمُخْلَصِينَ﴾

﴿*'illā 'ibāda llāhi l-mukhlaṣīn*[a]﴾

﴿*But they impugned him. So they will indeed be arraigned [before Him]—[all] except God's exclusive servants*﴾[288]

---

[287] Sūrat al-Ḥijr, Verses 39-40.

[288] Sūrat aṣ-Ṣāffāt, Verses 127-128.

And they deserve a reward far greater than their actions:

﴿وما تُجزَونَ إلّا ما كُنتُم تعمَلونَ﴾

﴿*wa-mā tujzawna 'illā mā kuntum ta'malūna*﴾

﴿إلّا عِبادَ اللهِ المُخلَصينَ﴾

﴿*'illā 'ibāda llāhi l-mukhlaṣīna*﴾

﴿*and you will be requited only for what you used to do—[all] except God's exclusive servants*﴾[289]

Hence, it could be argued that Sayyidah Fāṭimah's ﷺ most distinguished scholarly achievement is her capacity to accurately articulate the essence of God ﷻ, a privilege bestowed solely upon His devout servants:

﴿سُبحانَ اللهِ عمّا يَصِفونَ﴾

﴿*subḥāna llāhi 'ammā yaṣifūna*﴾

﴿إلّا عِبادَ اللهِ المُخلَصينَ﴾

﴿*'illā 'ibāda llāhi l-mukhlaṣīna*﴾

[289] Sūrat aṣ-Ṣāffāt, Verses 39-40.

﴾Clear is God of whatever they allege [about Him],—[all] except God's exclusive servants﴿[290]

The Ahl al-Bayt ﷺ can be likened to a wellspring of sanctity and heavenly wisdom, pouring forth like the Kawthar. Sayyidah Fāṭimah ﷺ serves as a channel for this wisdom, with her divine understanding and perception reflecting that of her equal, Imām ʿAlī b. Abī Ṭālib ﷺ. A few instances are cited below:

1. God's ﷻ blessings are unlimited and countless:

   "Praise be to God for what He has bestowed... countless in number and far from recompense in their duration, and transcending human understanding in their permanence."[291]

   These words of praise are similar to the famous praise uttered by Amīr al-Mu'minīn ﷺ:

   "Praise is due to God whose worth cannot be described by speakers, whose bounties cannot be counted by calculators and whose claim (to obedience) cannot be satisfied by those who attempt to do so."[292]

---

[290] Sūrat aṣ-Ṣaffāt, Verses 159-160.

[291] Ṭabrisī, Shaykh Aḥmad b. ʿAlī Ṭabrisī, *al-Iḥtijāj,* Vol. 1, p. 98.

[292] Sharīf Raḍī, Muḥammad b. al-Ḥusayn, *Nahj al-Balāghah*, Sermon 1.

The root of these two praises is the Noble Qur'ān:

﴿وَإِن تَعُدّوا نِعمَةَ اللَّهِ لا تُحصوها﴾

﴿*wa-'in ta'uddū ni'mata llāhi lā tuḥṣūhā*﴾

﴿*If you enumerate God's blessings, you will not be able to count them*﴾[293]

2. The understanding of God's ﷻ Knowledge transcends the realm of physical perception, and defining Him through language is unattainable, yet the human heart maintains a connection with these divine insights:

   "I bear witness that there is no deity except God, alone without partner, a word whose meaning is sincerity, embedded in the hearts, illuminating reason through reflection, inaccessible to vision, indescribable by tongues, and unimaginable in essence".[294]

   This outstanding description is equivalent to the famous description of Imām 'Alī ﵇ in which he says:

[293] Sūrat an-Naḥl, Verse 18.

[294] Ṭabrisī, Shaykh Aḥmad b. 'Alī Ṭabrisī, *al-Iḥtijāj,* Vol. 1, p. 98.

"Eyes cannot see Him face to face, but hearts perceive Him through the realities of belief."[295]

3. The inception of this universe is not derived from everlasting matter, nor is it founded on a pre-existing blueprint, nor is its purpose to attain an objective beyond the essence of the Creator, as each concept is constrained by human understanding:

"He originated things without any pre-existing matter and created them without following any examples. He brought them into existence by His power... without needing them for His creation or benefiting from their formation".[296]

This intellectual analysis of the system of creation from Sayyidah Fāṭimah ﷺ is almost identical to that of Amīr al-Mu'minīn's ﷺ:

"One who did not come into being from anything and was not created from something that had come into being before Him... He invented whatever He created without any examples to follow and without feeling overburdened or exhausted. All manufacturers manufacture things from something. God has not

[295] Sharīf Raḍī, Muḥammad b. al-Ḥusayn, *Nahj al-Balāghah*, Sermon 179.

[296] Ṭabrisī, Shaykh Aḥmad b. 'Alī Ṭabrisī, *al-Iḥtijāj*, Vol. 1, p. 98.

created whatever He has created from anything... Thus, I speak of my Lord."[297]

In this enlightening and Qur'ānic interpretation, the inherent eternity of God ﷻ and the dismissal of the concept of eternal matter were highlighted.

The fundamental point, articulated by these two infallible equals, along with other deep intellectual insights, led the late Shaykh Kulaynī ؒ to remark in conjunction with this sermon:

"This sermon is renowned... And it is sufficient for anyone seeking knowledge of monotheism if they contemplate it and understand what it contains. If all the tongues of humans and jinn, without a prophet among them, were to gather to explain monotheism in the same way that my father and mother ؑ did, they would not be able to do so. If it were not for his explanation, people would not know how to follow the path of monotheism. Do you not see his words: 'He did not originate from anything nor was He created from something that had previously existed.'""[298]

The revered Mullāh Ṣadrā ؒ, in honor of Shaykh Kulaynī's ؒ stature and elucidation of his words, states:

---

[297] Kulaynī, Shaykh Muḥammad b. Yaʿqūb, *al-Kāfī*, Vol. 1, p. 134-136.

[298] Ibid., p. 136.

> "Shaykh Kulaynī's statement implies that without a prophet among them, even if all men and jinns were to unite, they would be incapable of reaching such an understanding of monotheism."[299]

4. The imperative of resurrection plays a crucial role in individuals' moral development. Some adhere to God's ﷻ commands driven by their aspiration for paradise, while others abstain from sin out of fear of eternal damnation:

   "Then He made reward dependent on obedience to Him and punishment on disobedience to Him, to protect His servants from His wrath and to guide them to His paradise."

   This statement regarding the importance of the resurrection is similar to that of Amīr al-Mu'minīn's ﷺ:

   "...Certainly Paradise is the best reward and achievement, while hell is appropriate punishment and suffering. God is the best Avenger and Helper, and the Qur'ān is the best argument and confronter."[300]

---

[299] Mullā Ṣadrā, Muḥammad b. Ibrāhīm, *Sharḥ Uṣūl al-Kāfī,* Vol. 4, p. 47.

[300] Sharīf Raḍī, Muḥammad b. al-Ḥusayn, *Nahj al-Balāghah,* Sermon 83.

5. She articulates the necessity of revelation and the prophetic mission:

"Believers of false religions became divided into several groups serving their false gods, denied God ﷻ opposing the intrinsic nature. God ﷻ enlightened all these darknesses through my father, Muḥammad ﷺ."[301]

This discourse on the essentiality of the prophetic mission also carries the gravity of Amīr al-Muʾminīn's ؑ insightful declaration regarding the significance of revelation and the responsibility of prophethood, as he articulates:

"In this way ages passed by and times rolled on, fathers passed away while sons took their places till God ﷻ deputized Muḥammad ﷺ as His Prophet... At this time, the people of the earth were divided into different parties; their aims were separate, and their ways were diverse. They either likened God ﷻ with His creation, twisted His Names, or turned to someone other than Him. Through Muḥammad ﷺ, God ﷻ guided them out of wrong and with his efforts took them out of ignorance."[302]

---

301 Ṭabrisī, Shaykh Aḥmad b. ʿAlī Ṭabrisī, *al-Iḥtijāj,* Vol. 1, p. 99.

302 Sharīf Raḍī, Muḥammad b. al-Ḥusayn, *Nahj al-Balāghah,* Sermon 1.

Concerning the Noble Qur'ān and its illuminating teachings, a comparable assertion is echoed by these two impeccable figures.

The profound wisdom of many divine laws and guidelines is illuminated in the teachings of Sayyidah Fāṭimah 🌸[303], much like in the discourses of Amīr al-Mu'minīn 🌸. This includes his sermons on the fundamental pillars of faith[304], as well as his teachings on the principle of Imāmate of the Ahl al-Bayt 🌸[305]:

"They are the pillars of Islām and the refuge of adherence. Through them, the truth returned to its place, and falsehood was removed from its position with its tongue cut off from its root."[306]

6. Regarding the fight against oppression and falsehood, restoring the rights of the oppressed and raising one's voice against the oppressor are common themes found in the sayings of these two pure counterparts. Many examples can be found in the sermons of Amīr al-Mu'minīn 🌸, based on which if a state is not based on justice, it is based on ignorance regardless of their faith:

---

[303] Ṭabrisī, Shaykh Aḥmad b. 'Alī Ṭabrisī, *al-Iḥtijāj*, Vol. 1, p. 99.

[304] Sharīf Raḍī, Muḥammad b. al-Ḥusayn, *Nahj al-Balāghah*, Sermon 110.

[305] Ibid., Sermons 2, 3, 4, 87, and 93.

[306] Ibid., Sermon 239.

"You claim that we have no inheritance,

﴿أَفَحُكْمَ الْجَاهِلِيَّةِ يَبْغُونَ ۚ وَمَنْ أَحْسَنُ مِنَ اللَّهِ حُكْمًا لِقَوْمٍ يُوقِنُونَ﴾

﴾ʾa-fa-ḥukma l-jāhiliyyati yabghūna wa-man ʾaḥsanu mina llāhi ḥukman li-qawmin yūqinūna﴿

﴾Do they seek the judgement of [pagan] ignorance? But who is better than God in judgement for a people who have certainty?﴿[307]

Do they not know? Indeed, it has become clear to you like the shining sun that I am his daughter, O Muslims."[308]

"endure calmly the blinding darkness of tribulations... I watched the plundering of my inheritance."[309]

7. A Muslim who is free and follows the teachings of the Ahl al-Bayt عليهم السلام eliminates the outdated practice of tolerating oppression. This is because only an unjust individual would accept oppression:

---

[307] Sūrat al-Māʾidah, Verse 50.

[308] Ṭabrisī, Shaykh Aḥmad b. ʿAlī Ṭabrisī, *al-Iḥtijāj,* Vol. 1, p. 102.

[309] Sharīf Raḍī, Muḥammad b. al-Ḥusayn, *Nahj al-Balāghah,* Sermon 3.

"...The dishonorable cannot ward off oppression."[310]

and the consistent method of combating oppression is demonstrated in the examples set by Ahl al-Bayt ﷦:

"... And our obedience is the system of religion, and our leadership is a security from division."[311]

"... Islām revolves around us,"[312]

"And he certainly knew that my position about it was the same as the position of the axis about the hand-mill."

Although supplication serves as the believer's armor and weapon, the pillar of faith, the illumination of the heavens and the earth,[313] the remedy for all suffering,[314] and a beneficial cause for realizing desires:

"Supplication before God ﷻ for help is the means for its acceptance just as clouds are means of rain."[315]

---

[310] Ṭabrisī, Shaykh Aḥmad b. ʿAlī Ṭabrisī, al-Iḥtijāj, Vol. 1, p. 99.

[311] Ibid., p. 103.

[312] Sharīf Raḍī, Muḥammad b. al-Ḥusayn, Nahj al-Balāghah, Sermon 3.

[313] Kulaynī, Shaykh Muḥammad b. Yaʿqūb, al-Kāfī, Vol. 2, p. 468.

[314] Ibid., p. 470.

[315] Ibid., p. 471.

But the best supplication is that which is issued from a pure and pious heart,[316] and whose request is for perfection:

> "O my God, (please) grant me absolute devotion to You and illuminate the sights of our hearts with the light of observing of You, and arrive at the Core of Magnificence, and that our souls hang to the majesty of Your Holiness..."[317]

The mentioned matter regarding supplication and the conditions for its answering are found within many supplications from these two personalities. An important aspect of the supplication is the feeling of humility before God ﷻ. This blessing, like others, stems from a divine origin:

﴿وَما بِكُم مِن نِعمَةٍ فَمِنَ اللَّهِ﴾

﴾*wa-mā bikum min ni'matin fa-mina llāhi*﴿

﴾*Whatever blessing you have is from God*﴿[318]

---

[316] Ibid., p. 468.

[317] Sayyid b. Ṭāwūs, *Iqbāl al-A'māl*, Vol. 2, p. 687.

Qummī, Shaykh 'Abbās, *Mafātīḥ al-Jinān, Munājāt Sha'bānīyyah.*

[318] Sūrat an-Naḥl, Verse 53.

Sayyidah Fāṭimah ﷺ has, like her counterpart, mentioned this in her supplications:

> "... O Lord, make me consider myself low in my own eyes, and Your station Great in my eyes. Inspire me to obey You, act in a way that pleases You, and avoid what angers You. O kindest of the kind!"[319]

This is because selfishness acts as an intangible barrier. This barrier dissolves when one experiences a sense of humility before God ﷻ, revealing the splendor of God's Majesty. Simultaneously, a humble person perceives the elevation of God's ﷻ Grandeur within their soul. They strive to comply with God's ﷻ directives and seek to align their actions with what pleases Him while steering clear of what incurs His displeasure.

In conclusion, some extracts of the prayer of Sayyidah Fāṭimah ﷺ, which are almost identical to those of Amīr al-Mu'minīn's ﷺ, are to be recited after ẓuhr prayer:

> "Glory be to the One with the Lofty Majesty... Praise be to God ﷻ, by whose grace I have reached what I have reached in the knowledge of Him, acting for Him, longing for Him, and obeying His command. Praise be to God ﷻ, who did not make me deny anything from His book or be confused about anything from His

---

[319] Sayyid b. Ṭāwūs, *Muhaj al-Da'awāt wa Manhaj al-'Ibādāt,* p. 141.

Al-Amīn, Sayyid Muḥsin, *A'yān al-Shī'a,* Vol. 1, p. 323.

command. Praise be to God ﷻ, who guided me to His religion and did not make me worship anything other than Him."[320]

The grandeur of this praise, in its understanding and submission to God ﷻ, is evident. It leaves no room for doubt and embodies the essence of monotheism. It is linked with the denial of any deity other than the Sacred Being of God ﷻ.

This allows us to conclude about the flawless existence of this heavenly lady and the rationale behind her being named Fāṭimah, as stated by Imām Muḥammad al-Bāqir ؑ:

"When this lady was born, God ﷻ sent an angel to the Holy Prophet ﷺ so that he may name her 'Fāṭimah.'

Then he [the angel] said:

'He had set her free [*Faṭim*] with knowledge.'"

[320] Sayyid ʿAlī b. Mūsā b. Jaʿfar b. Ṭāwūs (Ibn Ṭāwūs), *Falāḥ al-Sāʾil wa Najāḥ al-Masāʾil*, p. 173.

Majlisī, ʿAllamah Muḥammad Bāqir, *Biḥār al-Anwār*, Vol. 83, p. 66.

Imām Baqir ؏ then said:

> "By God ﷻ! She was set free [*Faṭim*] with knowledge."[321]

This signifies that she was distanced from all forms of unawareness and negligence. May peace be upon her on the day she was born, her martyrdom, and the day of resurrection. O God ﷻ! Just as you hold affection for the Ahl al-Bayt ؏, grant us their love as well.

---

[321] Kulaynī, Shaykh Muḥammad b. Yaʿqūb, *al-Kāfī*, Vol. 1, p. 460.

Her Marriage and Family Life

The revered presence of Sayyidah Fāṭimah ﷺ and the diverse facets of her life resemble a radiant lamp illuminating the hearts of those seeking salvation and excellence. In a nutshell, the Islāmic viewpoint advocates for the optimal method of education, focusing on nurturing children and addressing their inquiries about religion. Similarly, it emphasizes aspects of marriage, as exemplified by the noble conduct of the Holy Prophet ﷺ.

In modern times, scholars in the field of educational sciences strive to explore both the apparent and concealed aspects of human psychological makeup and existential formation, including factors and challenges, to enhance educational disciplines. Reflecting on the stages of growth and development during the time of Sayyidah Fāṭimah ﷺ, we can deduce that despite the progress of science, her exemplary stature will perpetually endure as a guiding light for us to emulate.

Throughout her lifetime, Sayyidah Fāṭimah ﷺ encountered various aspects and domains of education in her pursuit of perfection, leveraging them to her utmost advantage. One of the most significant educational tools employed by this revered figure was her ability to instill inner motivation, affection, and a love for goodness and excellence in others. This love emanated from her innermost being and manifested in her actions and words. Her profound interest in fostering happiness in others profoundly influenced her character, captivating and inspiring observers and guiding them toward happiness. This is because love and affection are instrumental in attaining absolute perfection and serve as a path to salvation. Without love, one cannot reach their desired destination. Imām Muḥammad al-Bāqir ﷺ said:

> "Is religion other than love?"[322]

Hence, God ﷻ gave the reward for the prophetic mission to Sayyidah Fāṭimah ﷺ and the Ahl al-Bayt ﷺ:

﴿قُل لا أَسأَلُكُم عَلَيهِ أَجرًا إِلَّا المَوَدَّةَ فِي القُربىٰ﴾

﴿*qul lā 'as'alukum 'alayhi 'ajran 'illā l-mawaddata fī l-qurbā*﴾

﴿Say, *'I do not ask you any reward for it except love of [my] relatives'*﴾[323]

Without this love, all the Prophet's ﷺ efforts in guiding society and reforming the nation would be in vain.

In the lifetime of Sayyidah Fāṭimah ﷺ, every manifestation of love was a reflection of God's ﷻ Love, indicating that all forms of her affection were for God ﷻ. Hence, the infallibility and purity of the Ahl al-Bayt ﷺ leads individuals towards God ﷻ. Imām Ja'far al-Ṣādiq ﷺ has said:

---

322 Kulaynī, Shaykh Muḥammad b. Ya'qūb, *al-Kāfī*, Vol. 8, p. 80.

323 Sūrat ash-Shūrā, Verse 23.

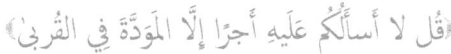

"If one's friendships, animosities, and gifts are for the sake of God ﷻ, they have attained the highest levels of faith, and their faith is perfected."[324]

This manner of showing love and affection captures eager hearts, subdues the flames of hatred and conflicts, cures depression, and renders life's most formidable challenges tolerable.

In addition to experiencing various aspects and influences of education, Sayyidah Fāṭimah (ʿa) had the guidance of the most accomplished teacher in human history, the Prophet Muḥammad ﷺ. She witnessed her devoted mother's compassion and patience during the prophetic mission's early years. She observed the affectionate demeanor of the Holy Prophet ﷺ towards his family. Through special gestures such as kissing her hands and publicly expressing his deep affection for her, the Prophet ﷺ laid the groundwork for love, loyalty, and emotional bonds in a world characterized by violence and brutality. In a society where burying infant girls alive was a prevalent custom, the Prophet ﷺ, through his conduct with his family, challenged this tradition, ultimately changing it.

Amidst a society marked by ignorance and disdain towards daughters, Sayyidah Fāṭimah (ʿa) experienced the utmost

[324] al-Barqī, Aḥmad b. Muḥammad b. Khālid, *al-Maḥāsin,* Vol. 1, p. 263.

Kulaynī, Shaykh Muḥammad b. Yaʿqūb, *al-Kāfi*, Vol. 8, p. 124-125.

affection from her father, which she then radiated towards others. This earned her the title of *Ḥāniyyah*, denoting her exceptional kindness and compassion towards her family. She was also known as *Ḥabībah* for her deep love for the Prophet of God 🕮, and as *Umm Abīhā* because to the Prophet 🕮, she was not just a daughter but akin to a mother. Sayyidah Fatimah 🕮 was equally benevolent and affectionate towards others, believing that

"The outcome of a believer's joyfulness is paradise."[325]

Her Sorrow and Devotion to Her Father

Sayyidah Fāṭimah's 🕮 deep bond with her father 🕮 stands out as one of the most prominent aspects of her life. On one occasion, when the Muslims were liberated from the economic blockade, the Prophet 🕮 was in prostration, engaged in conversation with his Lord, when some people from the Quraysh approached and placed the stomach of a camel on his revered head. Witnessing this appalling act, Sayyidah Fāṭimah 🕮 rushed forward to clean her father's face, yet her heart was heavy with sorrow at the sight of their mistreatment of him. For this reason, the Prophet 🕮 often remarked,

---

[325] Majlisī, ʿAllamah Muḥammad Bāqir, *Biḥār al-Anwār*, Vol. 72, p. 401.

"Fāṭimah is like an angel in human form. Whenever I wish to experience the fragrance of paradise, I find it in my daughter's scent."[326]

Sayyidah Fāṭimah ﷺ expressed:

"Upon the revelation of the verse:

﴿لا تَجعَلوا دُعاءَ الرَّسولِ بَينَكُم كَدُعاءِ بَعضِكُم بَعضًا﴾

﴿lā taj'alū du'ā'a r-rasūli baynakum ka-du'ā'i ba'ḍikum ba'ḍan﴾

﴿Do not consider the Apostle's summons amongst you to be like your summoning one another﴾[327]

I made a sincere effort to adhere to it. Consequently, I will no longer refer to him as 'father' but as 'the Messenger of God.' The Prophet said nothing for the first two or three times until he said:

'Oh Fāṭimah! This verse was not intended for you or my pure progeny. You are from me, and I am

---

[326] Ṣadūq, Shaykh Muḥammad b. 'Alī, *al-Amālī,* p. 461.

Majlisī, 'Allamah Muḥammad Bāqir, *Biḥār al-Anwār,* Vol. 43, p. 4.

al-Mīrzā al-Nūrī, *Mustadrak al-Wasā'il wa-Mustanbaṭ al-Masā'il,* Vol. 3, p. 156.

[327] Sūrat an-Nūr, Verse 63.

> from you. This verse has been revealed by the people of the Quraysh, who are cruel and arrogant. You should continue to call me 'father' as it brings joy to my heart and is also pleasing to God ﷻ.'"[328]

Despite this, when others addressed him as 'the Messenger of God,' his face brightened, and he responded eagerly, unlike when he was called by his name, to which he responded with indifference.

Sayyidah Fāṭimah ﷺ held a deep affection for her esteemed father, such that his presence always brought comfort to her, irrespective of the circumstances, as Aḥmad b. Ḥanbal records:

> "The Messenger of God, whenever he embarked on a journey, would make his daughter, Fāṭimah, his last visit. Upon his return, she would be his first. One day, upon returning from a battle, he, as usual, went to visit Fāṭimah. He noticed a curtain hung at the door and other alterations in the house's appearance. He immediately turned back, not setting foot inside. Fāṭimah quickly understood her father's sadness, removed the decorations and modifications she had made to the house, and sent them to her father."[329]

---

[328] Ibn Shahrāshūb, Muḥammad b. 'Alī, *Manāqib Āl Abī Ṭālib*, Vol. 3, p. 320.

[329] Ibn Ḥanbal, Aḥmad, *Musnad Aḥmad b. Ḥanbal*, Vol. 5, p. 275.

Fāṭimah had such a profound bond with her father that the thought of parting from him was nearly unbearable. This is why, following her father's demise, she was never again seen with a smile on her face. Her last smile was witnessed when the Prophet was on his deathbed, surrounded by his family. The impending death of the Prophet was most distressing for Sayyidah Fāṭimah, as she could not even bear the thought. As 'Ā'ishah recounts:

> "I have not seen anyone more akin to the Prophet than Fāṭimah. Her manner of speaking and conduct mirrored the Prophet's demeanor. Whenever Fāṭimah would enter the Prophet's presence, he would stand up out of respect, greet her warmly, kiss her hands, and make space for her beside him. On the night of the Prophet's death, Zahrā' had a private conversation with him. She was in tears, but upon hearing his whispered words, her face brightened, and she smiled. After the Prophet's death, I asked her why she smiled that day.
>
> She replied:
>
> 'The first time, my father said:
>
> 'Fāṭimah dear, I will be leaving you.'

Then he reassured me:

> 'My daughter, do not be sad. You will be the first one from my family to join me, and this brings me joy.'"[330]

Incorporating Poetry into the Process of Raising Children

Sayyidah Fāṭimah ﷺ imparted religious teachings through her actions, heartfelt worship, and abundant prayers, but also her considerate and affectionate conduct with her husband and father within the confines of their home. She employed the most effective educational techniques for child-rearing while practically instilling religious and ethical values. This esteemed woman would utilize even the smallest opportunities for education. Even when she sang lullabies to her children or engaged in play with them, she would, through poetry, contribute to their spiritual and physical development. For example, she would say the following to Imām al-Ḥasan ﷺ:

Ashbih abāka yā Ḥasan, wa-khlaʿ ʿanil-ḥaqqi rasan

Waʿbud lihā dhā minan, wa lā tuwāli dhāl-iḥan

---

[330] Ṭūsī, Shaykh Muḥammad b. Ḥasan, *al-Amālī,* p. 400.

Ibn Ḥanbal, Aḥmad, *Musnad Aḥmad b. Ḥanbal,* Vol. 4, p. 283.

al-Nisāʾī, Aḥmad b. Shuʿayb, *Sunan al-Kubra,* Vol. 7, p. 101.

Which roughly translates to:

> "Dear Ḥasan! Be like your father and remove the rope from the neck of righteousness. Worship the Benevolent God ﷻ and do not make friends with hostile and spiteful people."

When she would caress Imām al-Ḥusayn ؑ, she would say:

> Anta shabīh bi-abī, lasta shabīhā biʿalī

Which roughly translates to:

> "[Dear al-Ḥusayn] you are similar to my father and not your father ʿAlī." Imām ʿAlī ؑ would listen to these words of Fāṭimah ؑ and smile.[331]

A Kind Teacher

Sayyidah Fāṭimah ؑ would gracefully educate even the most ignorant and arrogant individuals. Her teaching style was so captivating that her students would declare that the time spent in her classes was the highlight of their day. Following is a report from one of Sayyidah Fāṭimah's ؑ sessions as narrated by Imām Ḥasan al-ʿAskarī ؑ:

---

331 Ibn Shahrāshūb, Muḥammad b. ʿAlī, *Manāqib Āl Abī Ṭālib*, Vol. 3, p. 389.

Ibn Ḥanbal, Aḥmad, *Musnad Aḥmad b. Ḥanbal*, Vol. 6, p. 283.

Once, a woman approached Sayyidah Fāṭimah ﷺ with a request. She explained,

> "My lady, my mother is elderly and in need, and she is unsure about certain religious rules related to prayer. She sent me to you to ask these questions and return the correct answers."

Sayyidah Fāṭimah ﷺ encouraged her, saying,

> "Go ahead and ask your questions."

The woman proceeded to ask her questions, one after another, and Sayyidah Fāṭimah ﷺ provided answers. After the tenth question, the woman felt embarrassed for asking so many questions and said apologetically,

> "Oh, daughter of the Messenger, I do not want to trouble you any further."

Sayyidah Fāṭimah ﷺ, with a smile, reassured her,

> "Do not hesitate to ask all your questions. If someone were hired to carry a heavy load from the ground to the roof for a thousand gold dinars, would they tire of the work?"

The woman replied,

"No."

Sayyidah Fāṭimah 🕮 said,

"I am like that hired person. God 🕮 has employed me to answer your questions, and for each answer, I receive a reward greater than a space filled with pearls between the earth and the sky. With such a valuable wage, why should I tire of answering? So, I will answer all your questions without feeling burdened."

She 🕮 then continued:

"I heard from my father who said: 'The scholars of our school [of thought] will be assembled on the day of judgment, will be clothed in heavenly garments of reflecting the vast knowledge they have gained and their efforts in guiding God's 🕮 servants. Each of them will be embellished with a thousand radiant veils."

Then, a divine proclamation will echo among the people of Maḥshar from God 🕮:

"Oh assembly, who have embraced the guardianship of the orphans from the family of Muḥammad. These are your worldly students, the same orphans you nurtured and enriched their lives with knowledge. They, in turn, educated others and clothed them in the garments of knowledge."

Following this, God ﷻ will command to amplify the rewards of such scholars and bestow upon them the highest honor.[332]

The Refuge for the Shīʿah

One of the characteristics of Sayyidah Fāṭimah ﷺ was her care for the Muslim nation, especially the Shīʿah of Amīr al-Mu'minīn ﷺ. It was such that whenever she would pray, she would put others before herself, akin to her father:

> "When Fāṭimah was praying, she would pray for the believing men and women, not for herself. When asked about this, she replied:
>
> "First, the neighbors, then the household."[333]

During Sayyidah Fāṭimah ﷺ's wedding, when the dowry was set and she was informed of the amount, she approached the Prophet ﷺ and said,

> "Oh Messenger of God! The dowry for others is in dirhams, so what sets mine apart? I ask that you return

---

[332] Imām ʿAskarī, Ḥasan b. ʿAlī, *Tafsīr al-Mansūb ilā Imām al-ʿAskarī,* p. 340.

Majlisī, ʿAllamah Muḥammad Bāqir, *Biḥār al-Anwār,* Vol. 2, p. 3.

[333] Ṣadūq, Shaykh Muḥammad b. ʿAlī, *ʿIlal al-Sharāiʿ,* Vol. 1, p. 182.

Majlisī, ʿAllamah Muḥammad Bāqir, *Biḥār al-Anwār,* Vol. 9, p. 388.

my dowry and request God ﷻ to make my dowry the intercession for the sinners of your Muslim nation."

Subsequently, Jibrāʾīl ؑ descended with a silk cloth in his hand, inscribed with the words:

"God has assigned the dowry of Fāṭimah al-Zahrāʾ as intercession for the sinners of her father's nation."

As she lay on her deathbed, she willed that this cloth be placed on her chest, saying,

"On the day of Judgement, I will rise with this cloth in my hand, and I will intercede for the sinners of my father's nation."[334]

Asmāʾ b. ʿAmays narrates:

"I was present in the last moments of Sayyidah Fāṭimah's ؑ life. That lady of knowledge performed the ritual bath changed her clothing, went to the corner of the house, and started whispering something in secret. I went forward to see what she was doing when I realized she was facing the Qiblah with her hands raised to the sky. She said with complete sincerity,

---

[334] Marʿashī Najafī, Sayyid Shahāb al-Dīn, *Sharḥ Iḥqāq al-Ḥaq*, Vol. 10, p. 376.

> "Oh my Lord! I ask you for by the right of the people you have selected, and by the cries of my two children when I am separated from them, forgive my Shī'ah and those of my children."[335]

Jābir b. 'Abdullāh Anṣārī recounts from the Prophet ﷺ:

"On the day of Judgement, my daughter will join the assembly, accompanied by a host of angels, radiating glory, honor, and respect.

A loud voice will then announce:

> 'Oh, people of Maḥshar! Close your eyes, for Fāṭimah, the daughter of Muḥammad, wishes to proceed.'

On that day, prophets, saints, elders, martyrs, and all of mankind will close their eyes as my daughter moves through the throng, enveloped in a halo of light, and arrives before God's ﷻ Throne.

There, she will plead:

> 'Oh my Lord! Protect my children, my Shī'ah, those who follow my children, and the friends of my children.'

---

[335] Iṣfahānī, Jawād Qayyūmī, *Ṣaḥīfat al-Zahrā'*, p. 210.

God ﷻ will then command:

> 'Where are the children, Shī'ah, and friends of Fāṭimah and her children?'

They will then step forward, encircled by angels, and Fāṭimah will lead them into heaven."[336]

Her Marriage Ceremony

Sometime after the blessed marriage of Amīr al-Mu'minīn ؑ and Sayyidah Fāṭimah ؑ, the Prophet ﷺ asked Amīr al-Mu'minīn ؑ:

> "How did you find your wife, Fāṭimah?"

He ؑ replied:

> "She is the best aid in the obedience and servitude of God ﷻ."

The Prophet ﷺ then asked the same of Sayyidah Fāṭimah ؑ, who replied:

---

[336] Ṣadūq, Shaykh Muḥammad b. 'Alī, *al-Amālī,* p. 17-18.

Majlisī, 'Allamah Muḥammad Bāqir, *Biḥār al-Anwār,* Vol. 43, p. 220.

"He is the best husband."[337]

When Sayyidah Fāṭimah 🌸 became Imām 'Alī 🌸's wife, they faced challenging circumstances, particularly in early Islāmic society. The Islāmic army was perpetually prepared for war, with several battles occurring each year, and her husband was always at the forefront. Upon his return from defending the Islāmic cause, he would be covered in wounds, and his clothes would be torn and bloodied. It was Sayyidah Fāṭimah 🌸 who would cleanse his body, tend to his wounds, wash his blood-soaked clothes,[338] praise his sacrifices, and uplift his spirits, readying him for the next battle. Moreover, their living conditions were extremely tough, especially during their initial years together. Despite the exhausting work in the gardens of Madīnah, Imām 'Alī 🌸 sometimes had no option but to take loans to sustain their livelihood, and there were days when they went without food. One day, when the Imām 🌸 came home exhausted after a hard day's work, the kindness and care from his wife made him forget all his hardships.

---

[337] Ibn Shahrāshūb, Muḥammad b. 'Alī, *Manāqib Āl Abī Ṭālib*, Vol. 3, p. 356.

Majlisī, 'Allamah Muḥammad Bāqir, *Biḥār al-Anwār*, Vol. 43, p. 117.

[338] Ibn Hishām, 'Abd al-Mālik, *al-Sīrat al-Nabawiyyah*, Vol. 2, p. 100.

The Imām ﵇ expressed,

> "Indeed, whenever I looked at her, all my worries and troubles would vanish."[339]

Contentment, Simplicity, and Gratitude

Salmān al-Fārsī (the Persian) narrates:

> "One day, I noticed Sayyidah Fāṭimah ﵉ dressed in simple attire with a veil on her head. I said to myself,
>
> > 'How strange! The daughters of the kings of Iran and the Roman emperor sit on golden thrones and wear luxurious garments, yet the daughter of the messenger of God ﷺ, whose stature surpasses them all, wears humble clothing."
>
> Sayyidah Fāṭimah ﵉ approached the Prophet ﷺ and said,
>
> > 'Oh messenger of God! My modest attire took aback Salmān. I swear by God ﷻ, who chose you for this divine mission that my husband 'Alī and I lead a simple life. Our home's carpet is made of

---

[339] al-Irdibillī, 'Alī b. 'Isā Hakkārī, *Kashf al-Ghummah fī Ma'rifat al-A'imma,* Vol. 1, p. 363.

Majlisī, 'Allamah Muḥammad Bāqir, *Biḥār al-Anwār,* Vol. 43, p. 134.

> sheepskin, a grazing spot for our camels during the day and our bed at night. Our pillows are leather sacks filled with palm leaves.'"[340]

Once, the Messenger of God ﷺ visited the home of Sayyidah Fāṭimah ﷺ and found his daughter seated on the floor. She was nursing her child with one hand while grinding wheat into flour with the other. Witnessing the humble yet fervent life of Sayyidah Fāṭimah ﷺ moved the Prophet ﷺ to tears. He said,

> "My daughter! Remember the sweetness of the afterlife and endure the hardships of this world."

Sayyidah Fāṭimah ﷺ responded,

> "Oh, Messenger of God! All praise and gratitude belong to God ﷻ for all the blessings He has given us."[341]

Avoiding Masculine Behavior

Imām Muḥammad al-Bāqir ﷺ narrated that Imām 'Alī ﷺ and Sayyidah Fāṭimah ﷺ sought the counsel of the Prophet ﷺ to enhance love and structure in their family

---

[340] Majlisī, 'Allamah Muḥammad Bāqir, *Biḥār al-Anwār,* Vol. 8, p. 303.

[341] Ibn Shahrāshūb, Muḥammad b. 'Alī, *Manāqib Āl Abī Ṭālib,* Vol. 3, p. 342.

Majlisī, 'Allamah Muḥammad Bāqir, *Biḥār al-Anwār,* Vol. 43, p. 86.

life. The Prophet ﷺ advised her to manage the household chores, while Imām ʿAlī ؑ was tasked with the responsibilities outside the home. Following this valuable advice, Sayyidah Fāṭimah al-Zahrāʾ ؑ expressed her joy, stating:

> "Only God ﷻ could comprehend the extent of my happiness. I am pleased because the Prophet's ﷺ guidance has relieved me from tasks typically associated with men."[342]

Humility and Compassion with Her Husband

Sayyidah Fāṭimah ؑ held a deep affection for her husband and empathized with him profoundly. When the caliphate's usurper sought an audience with her following the distressing incidents of Saqīfah and Fadak, Amīr al-Mu'minīn ؑ entered their home and informed her,

> "My dear, the two individuals are at the door seeking your permission to converse with you. What is your decision regarding this?"

Amidst her emotional turmoil and heartache, Sayyidah Fāṭimah ؑ responded with utmost humility,

---

[342] al-Ḥimyarī, ʿAbd Allāh b. Jaʿfar, *Qurb al-Isnād,* p. 52.

Majlisī, ʿAllamah Muḥammad Bāqir, *Biḥār al-Anwār,* Vol. 43, p. 81.

"Dear 'Alī, this is your home, and I am your wife. The decision rests with you."[343]

During a challenging time in their lives, the household of Imām 'Alī ﷺ was running low on food.

Imām 'Alī ﷺ inquired of his wife,

"Fāṭimah, is there a little food for us to eat?"

Sayyidah Fāṭimah ﷺ responded,

"By the Almighty ﷻ, who has elevated your dignity and respect, we have been without sufficient food for the past three days. I gave you the remaining morsels we had and bore the hardship of hunger myself."

Imām 'Alī ﷺ asked,

"Why didn't you let me know?"

Sayyidah Fāṭimah ﷺ explained,

"The messenger of God ﷺ instructed me not to ask anything from you and commanded,

---

343 Al-Ḥilālī, Sulaym b. Qays, *Kitāb Sulaym b. Qays,* Vol. 2, p. 869.

Majlisī, 'Allamah Muḥammad Bāqir, *Biḥār al-Anwār,* Vol. 28, p. 303.

'Do not request anything from my cousin. If he offers you something, accept it, but do not ask for it yourself.'"[344]

The Protector of Modesty and Chastity

Sayyidah Fāṭimah ؏ imparted a profound lesson to women about preserving their modesty and adhering to the ḥijab. On one occasion, a blind man sought permission to enter 'Alī's ؏ residence. As he arrived, Sayyidah Fāṭimah ؏ retreated behind a curtain and ensured her ḥijab was fully in place.

The Prophet ﷺ, who was present, questioned,

> "My daughter! He cannot see you, so why did you retreat behind the curtain to perfect your ḥijab?"

Sayyidah Fāṭimah ؏ responded,

> "Even if he cannot see me, I can see him, and he possesses the ability to smell."

The Prophet ﷺ then affirmed,

> "I bear witness that you are a part of me."[345]

---

[344] al-'Ayyāshī, Muḥammad b. Mas'ūd, *Tafsīr al-'Ayyāshī*, Vol. 1, p. 171.

[345] Al-Nu'mān, Abū Ḥanīfah, *Da'ā'im al-Islām*, Vol. 2, p. 214.

Throughout their shared life, Sayyidah Fāṭimah ؏ never acted in a way that would upset her husband. As she bid Imām ʿAlī ؏ farewell on her deathbed, she stated,

> "Oh beloved cousin! You have never found me to be dishonest or disloyal. Since we became companions, I have never defied your commands."

The Imām ؏ responded,

> "God forbid, your knowledge of God ﷻ, your generosity, your devoutness, your nobility, and your reverence for God ﷻ are so immense that there is no space for you to contradict me."[346]

---

[346] Nayshābūrī, Muḥammad b. Ḥasan al-Fattāl, *Rawḍat al-Wāʿiẓīn wa Baṣīrat al-Muttaʿiẓīn,* Vol. 1, p. 151.

Majlisī, ʿAllamah Muḥammad Bāqir, *Biḥār al-Anwār,* Vol. 43, p. 191.

Questions and Answers

1. With all her virtues, why was she not chosen as a prophet?

While a prophet is typically someone to whom divine revelations are made, it is not necessarily true that everyone who receives such revelations is a prophet. These revelations can sometimes be a message and, at other times, legislative.

The Noble Qur'ān elucidates the concept of legislative prophethood, manifested as a mission. This mission is an executive task that involves the masses and encompasses leadership in matters of war and peace, financial affairs, property distribution, and economic regulation. The Noble Qur'ān asserts:

﴿وَما أَرسَلنا مِن قَبلِكَ إِلّا رِجالًا نوحي إِلَيهِم ۚ فَاسأَلوا أَهلَ الذِّكرِ إِن كُنتُم لا تَعلَمونَ﴾

﴿*wa-mā 'arsalnā min qablika 'illā rijālan nūḥī 'ilayhim fa-s'alū 'ahla dh-dhikri 'in kuntum lā ta'lamūna*﴾

﴿*We did not send [any apostles] before* you *except as men to whom We revealed —ask the People of the Reminder if you do not know*﴾[347]

This implies that the mission is essentially an executive task for men.

---

[347] Sūrat an-Naḥl, Verse 43.

Hence, the mission involves leading a society, defining permissible, forbidden, obligatory, and recommended. It is a unique role, and being an executive position, it is entrusted to men. However, prophecy involves gaining knowledge through revelation about worldly matters, past, present, and future. This prophecy is rooted in wilāyat and is not associated with legislation or the executive mission. Although this type of prophecy supports any legislative mission, it is not exclusive to men, and women can also attain this position.[348]

2. Why is there only one woman among all the Prophets and the Fourteen Infallibles ﷺ?

It is not established that Sayyidah Fāṭimah ﷺ was the only infallible woman. There is no evidence to suggest that other women, such as Sayyidah Zaynab al-Kubrā ﷺ or Sayyidah Fāṭimah al-Maʿṣūmah ﷺ, were not also infallible.

The status of prophethood, the divine mission of wilāyat, infallibility, and the attainment of the *walī-Allāh* position are not exclusively male domains. There have been notable women, including Āsiyah, Sayyidah Maryam, Sayyidah Fāṭimah, Sayyidah Zaynab Kubrā, and Sayyidah Maʿṣumah ﷺ, who have potentially reached the position of wilāyat by preserving their status.

[348] Āmulī, Āyatullāh ʿAbd Allāh Jawādī, *Zan dar Āynah Jalāl wa Jamāl*, p. 167.

Therefore, the fact that all prophets are men does not necessarily imply that spiritual perfection is exclusive to men. Rather, spiritual perfection is reserved for the wilāyat of God ﷻ; in this respect, there is no distinction between men and women. Both genders are capable of achieving this status.[349]

3. Did all Righteous and Just Descendants of Prophet Ibrāhīm ؑ Reach the Position of Imāmate?

By the prayer of Prophet Ibrāhīm ؑ, all his virtuous and fair descendants attained the position of Imāmate. It is important to note that there are two kinds of Imāmate: Imāmat malakūtī, which is associated with the wilāyat, and Imāmat mulkī, which pertains to leadership and administration. The most significant role of Imāmat malakūtī is linked to the realm of beliefs, ethics, actions, and worship, which ascends to the spiritual world:

﴿إِلَيْهِ يَصْعَدُ الْكَلِمُ الطَّيِّبُ وَالْعَمَلُ الصَّالِحُ يَرْفَعُهُ﴾

﴾ʾilayhi yaṣʿadu l-kalimu ṭ-ṭayyibu wa-l-ʿamalu ṣ-ṣāliḥu yarfaʿuhū﴿

---

[349] Āmulī, Āyatullāh ʿAbd Allāh Jawādī, *Nasīm Andīshah,* Vol. 1, p. 83-84.

﴾To Him ascends the good word,
and He elevates righteous conduct﴿*[350]

Imāmat malakūtī is a spiritual path that requires a guide, a direct path, and a leader. This direct line represents the extended right between the servant and the Master.

Only the infallible is deemed fit to guide humanity in faith, ethics, and worship. In essence, the worship conducted by the Imām is considered the most superior form of worship, and the Muslim nation emulates it. The viewpoint of the Imām takes precedence over the opinion of the Muslim nation. It is said that an individual who prays at the prime time is imitating the Imām of his era because he prays at the prime time. However, the Imām might be where the horizon differs, so whoever offers the first prayer in the East and the West has followed the Imām of his era.

In the context of Imāmat malakūtī, morals, beliefs, actions, and, most importantly, human souls are interconnected with the faith, creation, and actions of the infallible Imām and are ascribed to him. These attributes belong to souls that aspire to ascend, and the infallible Imām guides such a journey. Hence, he is the Imām of souls, beliefs, and morals. Each of the infallible descendants of Ibrāhīm ﷺ possesses such an Imāmat malakūtī, with the most elevated

---

[350] Sūrat Fāṭir, Verse 10.

* Or 'righteous conduct elevates it.'

and notable belonging to the Ahl al-Bayt ﷺ, and Sayyidah Fāṭimah ﷺ is one of their most evident examples.

On the other hand, Imāmat mulkī, which pertains to leadership and administrative matters, as well as the divine mission and prophethood, necessitates interaction with humanity and their involvement in warfare. This aspect is specifically associated with men and not women.[351]

4. Why does the Prophet's ﷺ lineage continue through his noble daughter ﷺ?

In cultures with a religious orientation, the foundation of a small community, such as a family or clan, is a woman, signifying her significant role in society. For instance, the first verse of Sūrat an-Nisā' explains family:

﴿وَاتَّقُوا اللَّهَ الَّذِي تَسَاءَلُونَ بِهِ وَالْأَرْحَامَ﴾

﴿wa-ttaqū llāha lladhī tasā'alūna bihī wa-l-'arḥāma﴾

﴿Be wary of God, in whose Name you adjure one another, and the wombs﴾*[352]

[351] Āmulī, Āyatullāh 'Abd Allāh Jawādī, *Nasīm Andīshah*, Vol. 1, p. 88-90.

[352] Sūrat an-Nisā', Verse 1.

* That is, 'Be wary of God and observe the rights of the blood relations and beware of breaking the ties of kinship.'

However, at the beginning of the verse, the focus is on Man:

﴿يا أَيُّهَا النَّاسُ اتَّقوا رَبَّكُمُ الَّذي خَلَقَكُم مِن نَفسٍ واحِدَةٍ﴾

﴾yā-ʾayyuhā n-nāsu ttaqū rabbakumu lladhī khalaqakum min nafsin wāḥidatin﴿

﴾O mankind! Be wary of your Lord who created you from a single soul﴿[353]

But so that society is not assumed to be constructed by man alone, God ﷻ immediately refers to the creation of women from the same singular essence and then to the womb to make it clear that a large share of society's foundation stems from women, which is the axis of the family's formation.

The Noble Qurʾān's interpretation suggests that a small community is centered around women's compassion, not men's strength. Once established, the union of these small communities forms a larger society. Just as a clear sea cannot form from the collection of polluted waters, a utopia cannot emerge from many unhealthy or infected families.

---

[353] Sūrat an-Nisāʾ, Verse 1.

﴿يَخرُجُ مِن بَينِ الصُّلبِ وَالتَّرائِبِ﴾

﴿yakhruju min bayni ṣ-ṣulbi wa-t-tarā'ibi﴾

﴿which issues from between the loins and the breast-bones﴾[354]

What binds relatives together and makes them maḥram to one another is the womb of the mother, not the sperm of a man. Therefore, everyone's relatives are called arḥām.

The Noble Qur'ān says in this regard:

﴿يا أَيُّهَا النّاسُ إِنّا خَلَقناكُم مِن ذَكَرٍ وَأُنثىٰ وَجَعَلناكُم شُعوبًا وَقَبائِلَ لِتَعارَفوا﴾

﴿yā-'ayyuhā n-nāsu 'innā khalaqnākum min dhakarin wa-'unthā wa-ja'alnākum shu'ūban wa-qabā'ila li-ta'ārafū﴾

﴿O mankind! Indeed We created you from a male and a female, and made you nations and tribes that you may identify yourselves with one another﴾[355]

﴿تَبارَكَ الَّذي نَزَّلَ الفُرقانَ عَلىٰ عَبدِهِ لِيَكونَ لِلعالَمينَ نَذيرًا﴾

﴿tabāraka lladhī nazzala l-furqāna 'alā 'abdihī li-yakūna li-l-'ālamīna nadhīran﴾

---

354 Sūrat aṭ-Ṭāriq, Verse 7.

355 Sūrat al-Ḥujurāt, Verse 13.

﴾Blessed is He who sent down the Criterion to His servant that he may be a warner to all the nations﴿[356]

In the initial verse, both men and women are identified as the roots of small communities, but what unites them is the womb of women, not the sperm of men. In the subsequent verse, God distinguishes the cause of lineage but does not equate the two. Instead, He states that God created mankind from water and established familial ties through marriage. Marriage transforms non-maḥram relationships into maḥram, thereby applying the family law. This was echoed by the Prophet during the wedding of Imām ʿAlī and Sayyidah Fāṭimah, as well as by Imām Riḍa[357] at the wedding of Imām Muḥammad al-Jawād:

> "God incorporated the son-in-law into the lineage."[358]

In other words, the relationship becomes akin to blood relatives, and non-maḥram become maḥram, although not all relationship origins stem from this.

---

[356] Sūrat al-Furqān, Verse 54.

[357] Kulaynī, Shaykh Muḥammad b. Yaʿqūb, *al-Kāfī,* Vol. 5, p. 373-374.

[358] al-Irdibillī, ʿAlī b. ʿIsā Hakkārī, *Kashf al-Ghummah fī Maʿrifat al-Aʾimma,* Vol. 1, p. 349.

Majlisī, ʿAllamah Muḥammad Bāqir, *Biḥār al-Anwār,* Vol. 43, p. 119.

Therefore, children are acknowledged based on the verses of the Noble Qur'ān and historical records of each individual's descendants, whether through a daughter or a son. For this reason, the children of Sayyidah Fāṭimah 🌸 are recognized as the children of the Prophet 🌸.[359]

An historical testimony

During the debates with Imām Mūsā al-Kāẓim 🌸, Hārūn al-Rashīd posed numerous questions. One of them was:

"Why do you assert that you are the Prophet's heirs, when his uncle 'Abbās was still alive at his passing, thus it would not reach his cousin 'Alī b. Abī Ṭālib?"

Responding to Hārūn, who had previously acknowledged the caliphate of Amīr al-Mu'minīn 🌸, Imām Mūsā al-Kāẓim 🌸 stated:

"According to 'Alī b. Abū Ṭālib, in such a scenario, as long as a person's child is alive, only the parents and spouse can inherit. This applies whether the child is a boy or a girl. In this situation, the uncle does not receive an inheritance in the second tier of inheritors. The deviation that has arisen, which deprives a girl of her inheritance, has no basis in the Qur'ān. Instead, people from the tribe of Taym [of the first caliph], the tribe of 'Adī [of the second caliph], and then the

---

[359] Āmulī, Āyatullāh 'Abd Allāh Jawādī, *Tasnīm fī Tafsīr al-Qur'ān*, Vol. 17, p. 547-549.

Umayyads, for personal reasons, regarded the uncle as a father, contrary to the Qur'ān. Such an opinion was solely theirs. It is false and has no connection to the corpus of prophetic traditions."

Hārūn al-Rashīd continued to inquire:

"Why do you permit them to refer to you as the son of the Prophet, while you are the children of 'Alī b. Abī Ṭālib and the Prophet was only your maternal grandfather?"

Imām Mūsā al-Kāẓim ﷺ responded:

"If the Messenger of God proposed to one of your daughters, would you consent?"

Hārūn replied:

"Glory be to God ﷻ, why wouldn't I consent when it would be an honor for me."

The Imām ﷺ then stated:

"Understand that neither would the Prophet make such a request to us nor would we permit such a thing."

Hārūn asked:

"Why wouldn't you permit it?"

The Imām ﷺ answered:

> "Because the Prophet is considered our father and the father of our children, and as you know, the grandfather is maḥram to his granddaughters, while neither you nor your children have such a relationship with the Prophet."

Then the Imām ﷺ referred to a verse from the Noble Qur'ān:

﴿وَمِن ذُرِّيَّتِهِ دَاوُودَ وَسُلَيْمَانَ وَأَيُّوبَ وَيُوسُفَ وَمُوسَىٰ وَهَارُونَ ۚ وَكَذَٰلِكَ نَجْزِي الْمُحْسِنِينَ﴾

﴾*wa-min dhurriyyatihī dāwūda wa-sulaymāna wa-'ayyūba wa-yūsufa wa-mūsā wa-hārūna wa-ka-dhālika najzī l-muḥsinīna*﴿

﴿وَزَكَرِيَّا وَيَحْيَىٰ وَعِيسَىٰ وَإِلْيَاسَ﴾

﴾*wa-zakariyyā wa-yaḥyā wa-'īsā wa-'ilyāsa*﴿

﴾*and from his offspring, Dāwūd (David) and Sulaymān, Ayyūb (Job), Yūsuf (Joseph), Mūsā and Hārūn (Aaron) — thus do We reward the virtuous—and Zakariyyā, Yaḥyā (John), 'Īsā and Ilyās*﴿[360]

---

[360] Sūrat al-An'ām, Verses 84-85.

The Imām ﷺ asked:

> "Oh, Caliph! Who was the father of 'Īsā?"

The caliph replied:

> "He had no father."

Imām ﷺ then said:

> "The Noble Qur'ān recognized him as Ibrāhīm's child through his mother, Maryam. So understand that for this reason, we are considered as the children of the Prophet, through our mother, Fāṭimah al-Zahrā'."[361]

5. Is she exceptional or a realistic role model?

To address whether other women can attain the capabilities and virtues of Sayyidah Fāṭimah ﷺ, it is important to preface the discussion with a key point. The rules and characteristics of a woman fall into two categories: the first pertains to her inherent nature as a woman, which remains constant over time, such as the requirement of ḥijāb, chastity, and numerous other rules specific to women. The second category relates to the quality of education and upbringing. If women are raised with proper education, they do not differ from men in this respect. Any differences that may exist are not due to their gender.

---

361 Ṣadūq, Shaykh Muḥammad b. 'Alī, *'Uyūn Akhbār al-Riḍā*, Vol. 1, p. 81-84.

Suppose women, like men, can pursue academic fields and universities, study divine teachings, and acquire knowledge of a correct worldview, anthropology, the afterlife, and the correct method of spreading this message. Would the prophetic narrations still hold? Some narrations discourage seeking their advice, and others suggest their minds are deficient. Is this due to their nature as women or their education?

Imām ʿAlī ☙ states in a sermon about women:

> "Oh you who resemble men but are not men, your intelligence is akin to that of children, and your wit is comparable to that of the occupants of the curtained canopies [women kept in seclusion from the outside world]."362

In another statement, he ☙ says:

> "Do not consult women because their perspective is weak and their resolve is unstable."363

Do these types of narrations apply to women who are academics or researchers? Is it fair to suggest that their intellect is on par with that of children solely based on their gender? Or is their resolve in practical intellect weak and

---

362 Sharīf Raḍī, Muḥammad b. al-Ḥusayn, *Nahj al-Balāghah*, Sermon 27.

363 Ibid., Letter 31.

unstable? These misinterpretations are more likely based on the concept of male dominance, which has its roots in preventing women from receiving proper education and academic studies. If women were given the same opportunities as men, their merits would not be inferior to men's. In fact, since the Islāmic revolution of Iran, they have demonstrated their superiority in various fields.

In summary, the intelligence and capabilities of such women have a long history, and there are numerous historical accounts of their intellectual superiority compared to men. When Islām first emerged during a period of ignorance, recognizing its validity from a theoretical standpoint required reflection and intellect. Accepting it from a practical standpoint required strong determination to withstand any form of harm. Therefore, the individual who converted to Islām before others had a superior precedence and was considered virtuous, just as Imām ʿAlī ﷺ being the first man to accept Islām is considered one of his virtues.

Hence, it is important to acknowledge this and the wisdom of those women who embraced Islām before their husbands, discerned its truth through logical reasoning, and believed in it with unwavering resolve. At the same time, many men declined to accept it and sought to extinguish its light. For instance, Mālik b. Anas documents in his book that women adopted Islām while their husbands remained non-believers. This includes the daughter of Walīd b. Mughayrah, who was married to

Ṣafwān b. 'Umayyah, and Umm Ḥakīm b. Ḥārith b. Hishām, the wife of 'Ikramah b. Abī Jahl. Both these women pledged their faith to Islām prior to their husbands.[364]

6. How could she be tested before her creation?

Reflecting on the words from the ziyārah of Sayyidah Fāṭimah ﷺ that state:

> "Peace be upon you, oh tested one! Your Creator put you to the test before your creation, and you demonstrated patience and emerged victorious in His test,"[365]

Can we conceive such a trial? This query has been previously posed about the Imāms concerning their leadership by previous nations.

Our current state of existence is the ultimate and most inferior level, beyond which lies non-existence. This level is thus referred to as the physical world. Before this level, more potent and superior stages exist in their existential

---

364 Ibn 'Anas, Mālik, *Muwaṭa'a,* Vol. 2, p. 543-545.

Āmulī, Āyatullāh 'Abd Allāh Jawādī, *Zan dar Āynah Jalāl wa Jamāl,* p. 36-37.

365 Sayyid b. Ṭāwūs, *Jamāl al-Usbū',* p. 32.

Qummī, Shaykh 'Abbās, *Mafātīḥ al-Jinān, Ziyārat for Sunday.*

hierarchy. The creation order in these stages is determined by the strength and intensity of their existence, as the creation system in these stages differs from that in the physical stage—consequently, the notion of someone being created before their father is unproblematic.[366] In these stages, fourteen pure lights were created before all others, blessing others with their existence. This concept is highlighted in a narration from the Prophet ﷺ, who stated:

> "The first thing that God created was my light."[367]

It is narrated that once, while the Prophet ﷺ was amidst a gathering, Amīr al-Mu'minīn ؑ made his entrance. The Prophet ﷺ greeted him, saying:

> "Welcome to the one who was created forty thousand years prior to his father."

This prompted the question:

> "Oh, Messenger of God! Can a son be created before his father?"

---

366 The person who later becomes his father has no meaning in this stage of the physical world.

367 Ibn Abī Jumhūr al-Aḥsā'ī, Muḥammad b. Zayn al-Dīn 'Alī, *'Awālī al-La'ālī,* Vol. 4, p. 99.

Majlisī, 'Allamah Muḥammad Bāqir, *Biḥār al-Anwār,* Vol. 25, p 22.

To which he ﷺ responded:

> "Indeed, forty thousand years before Ādam, God ﷻ created me and ʿAlī from a single light, splitting it into two. He then formed matter from our light. Subsequently, He positioned us on the right side of His Throne. We then recited the tasbīḥ of God ﷻ, followed by the angels. We recited tahlīl [*lā illāha illallāh*] and the angels followed. We recited takbīr, and the angels followed. Thus, anyone who recites the tasbīḥ and takbīr is blessed by the teachings of ʿAlī."[368]

Such narrations, of which numerous examples, allude to the preceding stages of existence. Hence, the leadership of these noble individuals about past civilizations commences from those stages, of which this world is merely an echo. This analysis suggests that the former led to the latter, not vice versa. Furthermore, these narrations clarify their leadership about the angels, as their leadership extends to other realms of existence. If the angels, who are superior and more powerful, are under their leadership, then it is without a doubt that the Jinn are also under their leadership.

Nonetheless, the test referred to the esteemed lady, Sayyidah Fāṭimah ؑ, implies that the beloved daughter of

---

[368] Daylamī, Ḥasan b. Muḥammad, *Irshād al-Qulūb*, Vol. 2, p. 404-405.

Majlisī, ʿAllamah Muḥammad Bāqir, *Biḥār al-Anwār*, Vol. 25, p. 24.

the Prophet ﷺ underwent a form of test in the preceding stage that can only be interpreted in this manner. But what does this test entail? This is a discourse best left to its people, those with the capacity to comprehend it.

7. What is the ruling on bearing witness to her between the adhān and aqāmah?[369]

In relation to the recitation of the testimony:

أَشْهَدُ أَنَّ فَاطِمَةَ الزَّهْرَاءَ عِصْمَةُ اللهِ الْكُبْرَى، وَحُجَّةُ اللهِ عَلَى حُجَجِهِ

Ashadu anna Fāṭimatu-z-Zahrā' 'iṣmat-allāh al-kubrā, wa ḥujjat-allāh 'alā ḥujaj

between adhān and aqāmah after acknowledging the wilāyat of Amīr al-Mu'minīn ﷺ for the sake of rewards, several points are to be kept in mind:

1. Her infallibility is beyond question.
2. Her divine authority is indisputable.
3. The testimony above should be pronounced outside the prayer call, not within it.

---

[369] Āmulī, Āyatullāh 'Abd Allāh Jawādī, *Istiftā'āt*, p. 28.

Sayyidah Fāṭimah ؑ In Two Lights

A message for researchers of the Study of Sayyidah Fāṭimah ؑ[370]

In the name of God, the Beneficent, the Merciful

All praise and gratitude are due to God ﷻ, unbound by any through His Oneness, and is limitless in His Presence. Peace and blessings be upon the infallible messenger, particularly the final Prophet ﷺ, and blessings be upon Ṭāhā and Yāsīn, all of whom are reflections of the Noble Qur'ān, especially the Imām of our era ؑ. We express our deepest reverence for these individuals and dissociate from their adversaries.

The counsel of the divine guides bestows numerous practical and scholarly blessings, which are not confined to either men or women in their fundamental virtues. Thus, God ﷻ includes the name of Sayyidah Maryam ؑ among the ranks of other distinguished men. He ﷻ states:

﴿وَاذكُر فِي الكِتابِ مَريَمَ إِذِ انتَبَذَت مِن أَهلِها مَكانًا شَرقِيًّا﴾

﴾wa-dhkur fī l-kitābi maryama 'idhi ntabadhat min 'ahlihā makānan sharqiyyan﴿

[370] Āmulī, Āyatullāh 'Abd Allāh Jawādī, *Sarūsh Hidāyat*, Vol. 2, p. 133-142.

﴾*And* mentiọn *in the Book Mary, when she withdrew from her family to an easterly place*﴿[371]

As you are admirers of these reflections of the Noble Qur'ān and adhere closely to the Ahl al-Bayt in recognition of their status, and this illustrious assembly was established in the name of the mother of the Imāms, Sayyidah Fāṭimah, some crucial points must be acknowledged and will be outlined in several principles.

First principle: The perfection of a complete human lies in their universality, which transcends the physical realm and encompasses the entirety of the theology, cosmology, immaterial, and etymology realms. This unity may be possible and plausible if it is intact.

The Prophet's rank and those who mirror his soul are seen as a single entity, as exemplified by the statement,

"I am from al-Ḥusayn."[372]

These sacred entities represent absolute unity in the divine realm, yet they cannot embody God's Totality. However, in God's view, there is no multiplicity or duality among them:

---

[371] Sūrat Maryam, Verse 16.

[372] Mufīd, Shaykh Muḥammad, *Kitāb al-Irshād,* Vol. 2, p. 127.

Majlisī, 'Allamah Muḥammad Bāqir, *Biḥār al-Anwār,* Vol. 43, p. 261.

"Your souls, your light, and your form are identical; they are blessed, purified, and one of the other. God created you as lights and made you witness from His Throne."[373]

Regardless of the gender of this entity, just as morning and evening are subsets of day and night, in a state where there is no trace of day and night, concepts like sunrise and sunset cease to exist.

Moreover, gender is a characteristic that pertains to the physical body, not the soul, and it is inappropriate to assign gender to such an entity in a realm where there is no place for a finite or imperfect being; everything that exists does so in divine unity. There is a state of equality, harmony, and balance between Imām 'Alī and Sayyidah Fāṭimah. In this state of unity, which radiates like a candle, no one can even slightly compare to this. The differentiation between these counterparts is irrelevant, as no multiplicity among them would allow for assumptions of equality or inequality. When comparing them with others, it is also irrelevant as no individual will be deemed their equal, leading to the negation of the predicate.

---

[373] Ṣadūq, Shaykh Muḥammad b. 'Alī, *Man Lā Yaḥduruh al-Faqīh,* Vol. 2, p. 613.

Majlisī, 'Allamah Muḥammad Bāqir, *Biḥār al-Anwār,* Vol. 99, p. 130.

Qummī, Shaykh 'Abbās, *Mafātīḥ al-Jinān, Ziyārat al-Jāmi'ah al-Kabīrah.*

A clear aspect of comprehensiveness is ownership of the role of the caliphate and being entrusted with governance. In all these phases, Sayyidah Fāṭimah ﷺ, like Amīr al-Mu'minīn ﷺ, is recognized as God's ﷻ caliph and His absolute protector. However, the process of imamate and leadership, which carries executive duties, is specifically assigned to Amīr al-Mu'minīn, Imām 'Alī b. Abī Ṭālib ﷺ.

Second principle: The wisdom of Sayyidah Fāṭimah ﷺ mirrors that of the Noble Qur'ān, free from the impurities of sensory perception, fantasy, delusion, illusion, and imagination. This is because she, along with the entire Ahl al-Bayt ﷺ, is seen as the living embodiment of the Noble Qur'ān, as stated in Ḥadīth ath-Thaqalayn:

> "I will leave amongst you two weighty things, the book of God ﷻ and my progeny."[374]

Understanding the Noble Qur'ān requires a pure soul and heart, just as physical contact requires ritual purity:

﴿إِنَّهُ لَقُرْآنٌ كَرِيمٌ﴾

﴿*'innahū la-qur'ānun karīm*[un]﴾

---

[374] Ṣadūq, Shaykh Muḥammad b. 'Alī, *al-Amālī*, p. 415.

Majlisī, 'Allamah Muḥammad Bāqir, *Biḥār al-Anwār*, Vol. 24, p. 124.

﴿فِي كِتَابٍ مَكْنُونٍ﴾

﴿fī kitābin maknūn^(in)﴾

﴿لَا يَمَسُّهُ إِلَّا الْمُطَهَّرُونَ﴾

﴿lā yamassuhū ’illā l-muṭahharūn^a﴾

﴿This is indeed a Noble Qur’ān, in a guarded Book,*—no one touches it except the pure ones﴾[375]

The thoughtful acquire knowledge of the Qur’ān and the Ahl al-Bayt through conceptual understanding. This understanding necessitates the exploration of complex principles. To gain intuitive knowledge of these two divine entities, one must penetrate the veils of the immaterial and divine realms. Anything that obscures the observer's vision is also considered a veil for the seer.

Moreover, what an epistemology student perceives as a goal is merely a shell for an intuitive mystic, as he seeks an exemplar, not a concept. He pursues reality, not the mind, and he searches for a specific individual, not a general principle. The understanding that a conceptual interpreter and a mental observer gain from studying Sayyidah Fāṭimah's knowledge will not surpass the mental

---

[375] Sūrat al-Wāqiʿah, Verses 77-79.

* That is, the Preserved Tablet.

representation of Sayyidah Fāṭimah al-Zahrā' ﷺ and the manifestations of perfection, beauty, infallibility, purity, and similar attributes. The insights one derives from the verses of the Noble Qur'ān align with the reality of that lady, who, like the Noble Qur'ān itself, serves as an objective exemplar rather than a mental construct. She is an individual entity, not a concept, present witness, or mental construct. Even though she is likened to a rose, she is a witness to the prophets and saints, not merely a bystander. If an observer studying that noble lady presumes something and believes that he has grasped the entirety of the matter because it narrates reality and reflects the external world, not merely because it exists in his mind, he should reconsider his words. What he labels as reality or external, although they are indeed so in the primary sense, are mental and not objective. His only gain is the knowledge of reality, and he has only perceived it through the veil of its scientific form. The sole path to reach that known reality is to transition from the mental realm to the objective, to journey from the absent to the present, and ultimately, to move from the knowledge of certainty to the eye of certainty. Such a task is not straightforward for conceptual observers but is unique to objective seers.

With eyes of purity, he is viewed akin to the crescent's moon,

Each glimpse of that moon is but a fragment of it.[376]

---

[376] Ḥāfiẓ, Shams al-Dīn, *Dīwān Ḥāfiẓ*, Ghazal 72, p. 101.

The difficulty of knowing Sayyidah Fāṭimah ﷺ is that people are deprived and prohibited from knowing her. The following narration refers to this:

> "...because people have been distanced from acknowledging her wisdom [and insight]."[377]

Even for the many who have witnessed, her true essence will remain unseen.

Third principle: While all the infallible members of the Ahl al-Bayt ﷺ stem from the lineage of Ṭāhā and Yāsīn, signifying that this pure lineage is on par with the Noble Qur'ān, and each member embodies the divine words of God ﷻ; Sayyidah Fāṭimah ﷺ possesses a unique attribute not found in the other infallible beings. This lady was equivalent to the Noble Qur'ān and was its companion, associate, co-traveler, and co-voice. In such a manner, she and the Noble Qur'ān transitioned from perfection to the physical realm together and simultaneously bid farewell together as their natural life concluded; however, their essence, especially that of the Noble Qur'ān, endures eternally.

The explanation is that her sacred life began concurrently with the revelation of the Noble Qur'ān and concluded with its end. As her blessed life spanned less than twenty

---

[377] Furat b. Ibrāhīm, *Tafsīr Furat,* p. 581.

Majlisī, 'Allamah Muḥammad Bāqir, *Biḥār al-Anwār,* Vol. 43, p. 65.

years, while the period of revelation was nearly twenty-three years, it is noteworthy that before the revelation, the Prophet 🌸 ascended to the heavens, laying the groundwork for the formation of the revelation. This journey provided the heavenly seed later manifested as Sayyidah Fāṭimah 🌸. This indicates that the time between the start of the revelation and the birth of Sayyidah Fāṭimah 🌸 was a prelude to her birth, made possible only by the blessing of the Noble Qur'ān.

During this period, all worldly conditions were readied for this celestial lady to descend from the throne to the earth. The divine sustenance given to the Prophet 🌸 on the night of ascension materialized, coinciding with the revelation of the Noble Qur'ān's verses until they attained perfection. Subsequently, the verse was revealed:

﴿الْيَوْمَ أَكْمَلْتُ لَكُمْ دِينَكُمْ وَأَتْمَمْتُ عَلَيْكُمْ نِعْمَتِي وَرَضِيتُ لَكُمُ الإِسلامَ دِينًا﴾

*'l-yawma 'akmaltu lakum dīnakum wa-'atmamtu
'alaykum ni'matī wa-raḍītu lakumu l-'islāma dīnan*

*﴿Today I have perfected your religion for you, and I have
completed My blessing upon you, and I have approved Islām
as your religion﴾*[378]

And the sun of revelation began to set. The Qur'ānic revelation concluded with its clandestine burial. This was

---

[378] Sūrat al-Mā'idah, Verse 3.

the unknown Laylat al-Qadr, which distanced itself from the uninformed Muslim society, and on Laylat al-Qabr, it bid them goodbye.

Nonetheless, the truth of wilāyat has always paralleled the Noble Qur'ān, accompanying it on an everlasting journey. Just as the allegation of tampering with the Holy Book is unfounded, the assertion that

> "the Qur'ān is sufficient for us"[379]

is a perspective that yields no benefits. The one who clips the wings of the Ahl al-Bayt ﷺ from their understanding of religion will never benefit from the religion he claims to be Islām.

The essence is that while the spiritual endurance of wilāyat, infallibility, and being a flawless proof of God ﷻ, Sayyidah Fāṭimah ﷺ, akin to the Noble Qur'ān, is guaranteed, the visible life of the vocal and silent Noble Qur'ān was simultaneous at the start and conclusion of her life, in a manner that they nearly descended and ascended in unison.

Fourth principle: The central purpose of this assembly is to delve into the study of Sayyidah Fāṭimah ﷺ. This study encompasses the exploration of innate disposition—an understanding that transcends mere doctrinal

379 Bukhārī, Muḥammad b. Ismā'īl, *Ṣaḥīḥ Bukhārī,* Vol. 5, p. 138.

formulations. It spans ethical, legal, jurisprudential, and social dimensions. This knowledge extends to scientific principles and practical guidance for the complete human being, who serves as an exemplar for all. Consequently, it is crucial to present some of Sayyidah Fāṭimah's ﷺ statements related to ethical and legal matters, among others. Without such a presentation, the practical impact of comprehending her holiness remains incomplete.

Lack of knowledge reflects ingratitude,

Truth-seeking is the right of knowledge.[380]

Sayyidah Fāṭimah ﷺ eloquently conveyed the profound impact of sincerity in action. Her words resonate with wisdom and divine truth:

> "Whoever raises and elevates their sincere worship to God, God will send and reveal His best interests to them."[381]

These precious words find their roots in the verses of revelation:

---

[380] Shabistārī, Maḥmūd, *Gulshan-e Rāz*, p. 100.

[381] Imām 'Askarī, Ḥasan b. 'Alī, *Tafsīr al-Mansūb ilā Imām al-'Askarī*, p. 327.

Majlisī, 'Allamah Muḥammad Bāqir, *Biḥār al-Anwār*, Vol 67, p. 249-250.

﴿إِلَيْهِ يَصْعَدُ الْكَلِمُ الطَّيِّبُ وَالْعَمَلُ الصَّالِحُ يَرْفَعُهُ﴾

﴾ʾilayhi yaṣʿadu l-kalimu ṭ-ṭayyibu wa-l-ʿamalu ṣ-ṣāliḥu yarfaʿuhū﴿

﴾To Him ascends the good word, and He elevates righteous conduct﴿*[382]

Indeed, sincerity is not an isolated virtue; it intertwines with belief, behavior, and deeds. A pure heart, unburdened by ulterior motives, allows the believer to ascend toward God. The companionship of a sincere believer draws them closer to the Divine, with grace and greatness. Such a traveler, whose journey leads to the Creator, will find reasonable means to meet their needs on the difficult path to the afterlife.

Similarly, her sanctity acts as a beacon for discerning the proper ways to benefit from worldly life, a task which falls upon such a group of scholars to define and derive from. She expressed affection for three aspects of this world:

> "I love three things from your world: spending in the way of God ﷻ, reciting the Book of God ﷻ, and

[382] Sūrat Fāṭir, Verse 10.

* Or 'righteous conduct elevates it.'

> looking at the face of my father, the Messenger of God ﷺ."[383]

Every divine blessing carries an obligation, regarded as a contribution towards the path of God ﷻ, some mandated and some voluntary. The obligation for courage is jihād in the defense of Islām. The obligation for beauty is maintaining modesty and avoiding impurity. The fountainhead of all these divine blessings is the Noble Qur'ān, encouraged to be recited, contemplated, and expounded upon. Observing the authentic and authoritative figure of the Prophet ﷺ provides a warmth to the heart that bridges theoretical insights with actionable inspirations. Even if modern society misses out on the direct blessing of the Prophet ﷺ, it remains enriched by studying his enlightening and nurturing teachings.

Āyatullāh 'Abd Allāh Jawādī Āmulī

October 2002

---

[383] 'Aṭārudī, 'Azīzallah, *Musnad Fāṭimah al-Zahrā'*, p. 161.

A Message to the Congress: 'Lady of Light'384

In the name of God, the Beneficent, the Merciful

Praise be to God ☀, whose Unity renders all forms of idolatry detestable and invalidates any association. Peace and blessings upon the divine prophets ☀, particularly the Seal of the Prophets ☀, whose message dispels false prophets and whose successors, especially the Imām of the time ☀, stand proven and clear. Their divine appointment nullifies any secondary claims. We hold their holy personalities in utmost reverence and dissociate from their adversaries.

Before the scholars in the field and our fellow believers, we extend our honor to the scientific congress, 'Lady of Light.' We thank their diligent organization and acknowledge their past and present services. May they achieve continued success and blessings shortly.

On the auspicious occasion of the birth anniversary of Sayyidah Fāṭimah ☀, we extend our heartfelt greetings to the sacred abode of the Seal of the Prophet ☀ and all devoted seekers of the Noble Qurʾān and the Ahl al-Bayt ☀. May this blessed occasion fulfill the nation's individual and collective needs and shine forth with the radiance of unity within the Islāmic community.

---

384 Āmulī, Āyatullāh ʿAbd Allāh Jawādī, *Sarūsh Hidāyat*, Vol. 2, p. 153-169.

While the intellectual scholars of the region have introduced Fāṭimi teachings, their efforts have significantly contributed to the objectives of the scientific conference. Nonetheless, some of the impacts of the esteemed lady, which are outlined in this message, are implicitly assured through adherence to these principles:

First principle: By understanding the essence of God's names ﷻ, Sayyidah Fāṭimah ﷺ attained a position as a representative of God ﷻ. Her identity encapsulated all the central elements of successorship: the destiny of Āl-'Imrān, the Verse of Muwaddat (a reward of the prophetic mission), the selfless act of feeding the needy, orphans, and captives, and the divine specification of the Kawthar. These elements collectively demonstrate her worthiness of revelation and her reception of the Muṣḥaf, which contained knowledge of the past and the unseen. Ordinary people find it challenging to comprehend such an extraordinary individual:

> "...because the people have been distanced from acknowledging her wisdom [and insight]."[385]

Therefore, what is beyond one's capacity is not commanded, and that which is dutybound is not possible.

---

[385] Furat b. Ibrāhīm, *Tafsīr Furat,* p. 581.

Majlisī, 'Allamah Muḥammad Bāqir, *Biḥār al-Anwār,* Vol. 43, p. 65.

Understanding the importance of knowing this 'Lady of Light' ﷺ arises from the duty to love the Ahl al-Bayt ﷺ. Love cannot truly exist without knowledge and comprehension. The deeper our understanding, the more profound our affection for that individual becomes.

Second principle: Sayyidah Fāṭimah ﷺ, described by infallible personalities, embodies the essence of Laylat al-Qadr[386] – a night symbolizing the evolutionary process of Islām and the remarkable leap taken by the true bearers of the Noble Qur'ān and the Ahl al-Bayt ﷺ. King Sulaymān (Solomon) ﷺ, who commanded the wind with majesty:

﴿الرِّيحَ غُدُوُّها شَهرٌ وَرَواحُها شَهرٌ﴾

﴾r-rīḥa ghuduwwuhā shahrun wa-rawāḥuhā shahrun﴿

﴾[We subjected] the wind: its morning course was a month's journey and its evening course was a month's journey﴿[387]

Was constrained by its limited speed. However, in the realm of the Prophet ﷺ, rank was determined by the crescent moon:

---

[386] Ibid.

[387] Sūrat Saba', Verse 12.

﴿لَيلَةُ القَدرِ خَيرٌ مِن أَلفِ شَهرٍ﴾

﴿*laylatu l-qadri khayrun min 'alfi shahr*[in]﴾

﴿*The Night of Ordainment is better than a thousand months*﴾[388]

This leap transcended time, allowing one to traverse a century in a single night. The measure of this extraordinary journey lies in the hands of the allies of Sayyidah Fāṭimah's ﷺ wilāyat, who diligently seek to comprehend this profound night. Thus, the concept of the Laylat al-Qabr (the night of burial) unfolding conventionally becomes inconceivable:

Now you are the Laylat al-Qabr,

go and become the Laylat al-Qadr.

As the measure of souls,

it becomes the core of revelation.[389] [390]

---

[388] Sūrat al-Qadr, Verse 3.

[389] Balkhī, Jalāl al-Dīn, *Kuliyāt Dīwān Shams*, p. 798.

[390] Ed.: Why? Because when you become a Laylat al-Qadr, you become the nest and abode of the souls of the angels instead of just being the abode of attachments and needs.

During the ascension, the Prophet's ﷺ mount was the Mi'rāj, which left a trail of light with every step:

> "and its steps were as far as its eyes could extend to."[391]

Similarly, prayer serves as a guiding beacon for the Muslim community, standing upright in alignment with the faith. When performed correctly, it reveals the essence of the Laylat al-Qadr. At this spiritual height, one can perceive the Qadr, a platform for ascension, reaching up to the stature to visit Sayyidah Fāṭimah عليها السلام, by one's capacity:

I saw that king at dawn on the path,

'Has the Time Come?'

In the sleep of negligence, unaware of Him,

the highest of the high.[392]

But the lineage of Ṭāhā and Yāsīn performs its task as the noble lady عليها السلام introduces the family of purification herself in the sermon of Fadak, saying:

> "... So, praise be to God ﷻ, by whose Greatness and Light, those in the heavens and the earth seek means to Him. We are His means in His creation, we are His

---

391 Kulaynī, Shaykh Muḥammad b. Ya'qūb, *al-Kāfī,* Vol. 8, p. 376.

392 Balkhī, Jalāl al-Dīn, *Kuliyāt Dīwān Shams*, p. 17.

special and holy station, we are His evidence in His absence, and we are the heirs of His prophets."[393]

The valid and anticipated outcome of tawassul is not about God ﷻ becoming closer to His servant through a medium, nor about Him paying heed to their words because of it, nor about His ability to fulfill their needs to the extent that it is said that God ﷻ is

﴿وَنَحْنُ أَقْرَبُ إِلَيْهِ مِنْ حَبْلِ الْوَرِيدِ﴾

﴾wa-naḥnu 'aqrabu 'ilayhi min ḥabli l-warīdi﴿

﴾and We are nearer to him than his jugular vein﴿[394]

or that God ﷻ

﴿عَلَىٰ كُلِّ شَيْءٍ قَدِيرٌ﴾

﴾'alā kulli shay'in qadīrun﴿

﴾has power over all things﴿[395]

---

[393] al-Ṭabarī, Muḥammad b. Jarīr, *Dalā'il al-Imāmat,* p. 113-114.

[394] Sūrat al-Qāf, Verse 16.

[395] Sūrat al-Baqarah, Verse 20.

Instead, tawassul implies that the servant's wishes are considered and their needs are addressed. Ultimately, initiating tawassul originates from God ﷻ Himself:

﴿وَابْتَغُوا إِلَيْهِ الْوَسِيلَةَ﴾

﴾*wa-btaghū 'ilayhi l-wasīlata*﴿

﴾*and seek the means of recourse to Him*﴿[396]

The responsibility and capability to ascertain the means of this tawassul does not lie with the general public. Instead, it necessitates an external elucidation and cannot be comprehended solely from the verse. In her sermon, Sayyidah Fāṭimah (a) indicates that the Ahl al-Bayt (a) serves as one of these means of tawassul.

Third principle: Through her actions and the traditions of the infallible Ahl al-Bayt (a), Sayyidah Fāṭimah (a) emerged as a role model for all of humanity. Yet, she exhibited unique behaviors specific to her, such as her inward spiritual journey, her constant mindfulness, her mystical way of life, and her thought process. These examples are particularly relevant to mystics, theologians, jurists, and specialists. The analysis of her renowned sermon serves as a testament to the authority of the most learned expert in intellectual sciences and transmission. For example, the statement:

---

[396] Sūrat al-Mā'idah, Verse 35.

> "He created things not from anything that existed before."[397]

This assertion is a robust rebuttal to some of the arguments put forth by atheists, who primarily question:

> "If the world has an effective origin and if that origin created something, was its first creation derived from existence or non-existence?"

The raw material of this world is eternal, does not necessitate an origin, and was created from non-existence. However, if it were created from nothingness, it does not possess the capability to create matter, leading us to the principle of the impossibility of the coexistence and absence of contradictions.

To clarify this uncertainty, the language used in this enlightening sermon did not involve the contradiction of existence and non-existence. Instead, the phrase used was "not from that which existed before." Simply put, God ﷻ brought the world into being without relying on anything that existed beforehand. This specialized terminology, originating from these infallible teachers of wisdom, became the scientific heritage of Imām 'Alī ﷺ following Sayyidah Fāṭimah ﷺ and was reflected in his sermons. These groundbreaking intellectual principles, which form

---

[397] al-Ṭabarī, Muḥammad b. Jarīr, *Dalā'il al-Imāmat,* p. 111.

Ṭabrisī, Shaykh Aḥmad b. 'Alī Ṭabrisī, *al-Iḥtijāj,* Vol. 1, p. 98.

the foundation of mystical and theological thought, were also present in the declarations of the Lady of Light ﷺ. The Verses of Inheritance, their communication to the public, and their specific application to the members of the Ahl al-Bayt ﷺ could be a topic of discussion for legal scholars and commentators whose writings fall within the purview of this message.

Fourth principle: Sayyidah Fāṭimah ﷺ affirmed the importance of diversity and political and social pluralism, all while upholding the core principle of unity and the need for unity and collaboration within the Muslim community, per prophetic traditions. She steered clear of any internal conflict and regional disputes, and, following the example of Amīr al-Mu'minīn ﷺ, she strictly avoided causing any divisions among Muslims. She believed that fortifying the Islāmic system against foreign adversaries was crucial.

To summarize, there is no room for pluralism within the framework of Islām, implying that there are numerous direct routes and everyone can reach their desired destination through various paths. Similarly, there is no pluralism in accurate knowledge, ensuring its correctness and relativity. Any interpretation from religious text should be accurate, and there is no space for pluralistic differences in this context. Therefore, due to differing opinions, theological debates will always remain relevant, as truth will emerge in such judicious and fair discussions. However, political diversity at the global and social levels within specific areas and peaceful coexistence among various tendencies and diverse beliefs are both logical and acceptable and will thus be accepted.

The life of the infallible Ahl al-Bayt ﷺ, with Sayyidah Fāṭimah ﷺ as a notable figure, aligns with the Noble Qurʾān, paralleling it in significance. For followers of this faith, there is a specific guideline:

﴿إِنَّمَا الْمُؤْمِنُونَ إِخْوَةٌ﴾

﴿innamā l-muʾminūna ʾikhwatun﴾

﴿The faithful are indeed brothers﴾[398]

There are also guidelines for followers of Abrahamic religions:

﴿يَا أَهْلَ الْكِتَابِ تَعَالَوْا إِلَىٰ كَلِمَةٍ سَوَاءٍ بَيْنَنَا وَبَيْنَكُمْ﴾

﴿yā-ʾahla l-kitābi taʿālaw ʾilā kalimatin sawāʾin baynanā wa-baynakum﴾

﴿O People of the Book! Come to a word common between us and you﴾[399]

---

[398] Sūrat al-Ḥujurāt, Verse 10.

[399] Sūrat Āl ʿImrān, Verse 64.

Furthermore, there are guidelines for all other religions:

﴿لَا يَنْهَاكُمُ اللَّهُ عَنِ الَّذِينَ لَمْ يُقَاتِلُوكُمْ فِي الدِّينِ وَلَمْ يُخْرِجُوكُم مِّن دِيَارِكُمْ أَن تَبَرُّوهُمْ وَتُقْسِطُوا إِلَيْهِمْ ۚ إِنَّ اللَّهَ يُحِبُّ الْمُقْسِطِينَ﴾

﴿lā yanhākumu llāhu ʿani lladhīna lam yuqātilūkum fī d-dīni wa-lam yukhrijūkum min diyārikum ʾan tabarrūhum wa-tuqsiṭū ʾilayhim ʾinna llāha yuḥibbu l-muqsiṭīn[a]﴾

﴿God does not forbid you in regard to those who did not make war against you on account of religion and did not expel you from your homes, that you deal with them with kindness and justice. Indeed God loves the just﴾[400]

When Islām advocates for the establishment of justice and peace and extends an invitation of goodness to non-Muslims, it does not promote disunity among the believers who share a faith in one God ﷻ, one religion, one Qurʾān, and one qiblah, among other similar teachings. This is because such a divine book delves into topics like the unseen and martyrdom, fosters wisdom, and never encourages imprudent actions. Differences and disunity yield no benefits and are rooted in ignorance:

400 Sūrat al-Mumtaḥanah, Verse 8.

﴿تَحْسَبُهُمْ جَمِيعًا وَقُلُوبُهُمْ شَتَّىٰ ۚ ذَٰلِكَ بِأَنَّهُمْ قَوْمٌ لَا يَعْقِلُونَ﴾

*tahsabuhum jamī‘an wa-qulūbuhum shattā dhālika bi-
’annahum qawmun lā ya‘qilūna*

*You suppose them to be a body, but their hearts are
disunited. That is because they are a lot who do not apply
reason*[401]

If there is a tendency towards division, it will always serve
the enemy's interests and never benefit those who are
divided. This is evident in the profound and eloquent
speech of Imām ‘Alī b. Abī Ṭālib :

> "You should therefore avoid change in the matter of
> God's religion for your unity in respect of a right
> which you dislike is better than your scattering away in
> respect of a wrong that you like. Certainly, God has
> not given any person, whether among the dead or those
> who survive, any good from separation."[402]

This all-encompassing interpretation of the past, present,
and future demonstrates the establishment of God's
absolute tradition that there is no virtue in discord and
division. Where there is no virtue, there will only be vice,
and the root of all vice is arrogance.

---

[401] Sūrat al-Ḥashr, Verse 14.

[402] Sharīf Raḍī, Muḥammad b. al-Ḥusayn, *Nahj al-Balāghah*,
Sermon 176.

Fifth principle: Sayyidah Fāṭimah ﷺ serves as a beacon for those who seek truth, particularly women and in fields related to women. Both the Noble Qur'ān and the Ahl al-Bayt ﷺ, the two weighty things (thaqalayn), are fountains of practical and scientific knowledge. This role model is comparable to an ageless antique, resistant to wear and tear and devoid of deception; it does not lead to stagnation. Even when the analysis is influenced by prejudice and differing opinions, it remains grounded in a fixed principle. A book that purports to bestow life cannot resonate with a closed heart, a hardened soul, or a stagnant mind. Moreover, a book that advocates stability and permanence opposes time and decay. Instead, its significance is contingent upon the rational assessment in the light of Islāmic law.

It is important to recognize that, first and foremost, religion is a decree from God ﷻ. Secondly, the origin of religion is the eternal knowledge and the will of God's ﷻ Divine Essence. Thirdly, the revealers of God's decree (religion) are based on evidence or authentic narrations. Fourthly, evidence-based reasoning includes empirical and intellectual reflection devoid of analogies, illusions, and assumptions and is not tainted by these imperfections. Thus, it would not be reliable proof. Fifthly, authentic narrations include the Noble Qur'ān or prophetic narrations in such a way that the erroneous slogan of "the Qur'ān is sufficient for us"[403] is dismissed just like the

[403] Bukhārī, Muḥammad b. Ismā'īl, *Ṣaḥīḥ Bukhārī,* Vol. 5, p. 138.

ominous claim of a distorted Qur'ān. Sixthly, the revealers of the traditions of the Ahl al-Bayt ﷺ are reports based on consensus or popularity. These reports are either singular or validated reports with multiple chains of narrations.

In validating proofs, a part of jurisprudence principles, certain imbalanced disputes are avoided, and every argument is validated. For instance, the conflict between tradition and consensus will be bypassed, as consensus never contradicts prophetic traditions, and its legitimacy is based on the fact that it uncovers the tradition rather than being the tradition itself — and it is always rooted in religious textual evidence. Therefore, instances of discord between logic and religion are not feasible, as logical arguments employed in deduction are used for transmitted text, not on religion itself, against hearsay, and not Islāmic law. Thus, it should not be stated that a certain matter was proven by reason, while transmitted texts proved another.

Sound intellectual reasoning establishes or subjects a rule if a matter is validated. In both scenarios, it is subject to the discretion of the lawgiver, and in the afterlife, it will be either rewarded or penalized. Such a matter is undoubtedly religious and lawful. Through such an analysis, numerous criticisms are addressed, such as the establishment of the Islāmic government, the elucidation of religious management, and local, regional, and international laws. Because when the position of reason and consensus is affirmed, its legitimacy is also achieved. This is safeguarded from the fallacy and harm of logical analogy, grounded on jurisprudential principles, and shielded from conflict. This applies whether the authenticity of transmissions is verified or the integrity of the text, and from an external viewpoint, ensuring it remains protected from any conflict with definitive reason. In such a scenario, the rise and evolution of any evolution that aligns with religion is feasible.

The responsibility of crafting the discourse on the harmony between evolution and religion lies with the scholars of the Noble Qur'ān and prophetic traditions, as well as the experts in various wisdom and theological sciences. In this scenario, it would not be solely governed by pure text or restricted by the tyranny of mere reason. It would resemble the angels who perceive prophetic traditions and, through reason and narration, soar towards it, as stated by Imām Ja'far al-Ṣādiq :

> "God has bestowed two types of authority upon man."[404]

He is guided by articulate reason that invariably adheres to the necessity of revelation, and, in the certainty of compliance, he issues a ruling that must be obeyed. This implies that the dependability of a lasting religion is the evolution of its religious rulings, which are observant of religious texts, not standalone. This directive has been conveyed to us through the Ahl al-Bayt :

---

[404] Kulaynī, Shaykh Muḥammad b. Ya'qūb, *al-Kāfī*, Vol. 1, p. 16.

"We must establish the principles for you, and you must derive from them."[405]

Hence, a dedicated mujtahid never strays from deriving from these revealed principles and does not experience an identity crisis. He does not confuse the derivation process with the inception and establishment of a principle, which is a condemnable deviation. As a result, he does not prioritize evolution over religion.

Sixth principle: Sayyidah Fāṭimah ﷺ and the rest of the Ahl al-Bayt ﷺ have consistently followed the righteous path and have never erred in their interpretations. She has demonstrated resilience and triumph on her journey, even when it is sharper than a sword's edge. Similar to the Noble Qur'ān, she is safeguarded from distortion.

Honoring the birth of the lady of light, Sayyidah Fāṭimah ﷺ, clarifies the unfound arguments of humanism and feminism against Islām and eliminates the threat of discrimination between men and women. Although a scientific certainty in this regard is not straightforward, it is possible to speculate on this topic through a historical lens. Some have believed in the lack of man's control over their fate and decisions, ignoring the role of personal responsibility. This led others to think solely on their

---

[405] al-Ḥillī, Muḥammad b. Aḥmad b. Idrīs, *al-Sarā'ir al-Hāwā li-Taḥrīr al-Fatawī,* Vol. 3, p. 575

Majlisī, 'Allamah Muḥammad Bāqir, *Biḥār al-Anwār,* Vol. 2, p. 245.

terms, ignoring fate. This second group saw humans as the ultimate judges of right or wrong, true or false, good or evil, and beautiful or ugly, claiming absolute freedom as their right. It is possible to assume that the weakening of women in society and their exclusion from the sphere of politics was due to this rise of extremism and hence led to the birth of feminism. However, there is no solid proof for this assumption.

The Noble Qur'ān, in par with the Ahl al-Bayt عليهم السلام, bestows honor upon all of humanity, regardless of gender, as stated in the verse:

﴿وَلَقَد كَرَّمنا بَني آدَمَ﴾

﴿wa-la-qad karramnā banī 'ādama﴾

﴿Certainly We have honored the Children of Ādam[406]

It attributes its esteemed status to the divine viceroy, as expressed in the verse:

﴿إِنّي جاعِلٌ فِي الأَرضِ خَليفَةً﴾

﴿'innī jā'ilun fī l-'arḍi khalīfatan﴾

[406] Sūrat al-Isrā', Verse 70.

﴾*Indeed I am going to set a viceroy on the earth*﴿[407]

A viceroy or caliphate enforces the law given to him, not based on his personal preferences. Otherwise, he would be removed from this divine position and stripped of his high status and dignity. This position over mankind is rooted in the essence of God's ﷻ singularity, which is not tied to a specific gender. The arrival of all Prophets ﷺ, who was sent to convey the book of wisdom and perfection, all point back to this singularity, not their moral perfection and masculinity is not a prerequisite.

Certainly, in practical and executive tasks that involve the physical body, the boundaries are entirely different, and the established laws and regulations are separate. Some of these specific rules for women are highlighted to clarify that the spiritual laws about the soul should not be mixed with the physical body's laws, as there is no concept of equality in the physical sense. For instance, in the distribution of inheritance, despite some women receiving a smaller share, the Noble Qur'ān states:

﴿لا تَدرونَ أَيُّهُم أَقرَبُ لَكُم نَفعًا﴾

﴾*lā tadrūna 'ayyuhum 'aqrabu lakum naf'an*﴿

[407] Sūrat al-Baqarah, Verse 30.

﴿you do not know which of them is likelier to be beneficial for you﴾[408]

Similarly, it advises women about their speech:

﴿فَلَا تَخْضَعْنَ بِالْقَوْلِ فَيَطْمَعَ الَّذِي فِي قَلْبِهِ مَرَضٌ﴾

﴿fa-lā takhḍaʿna bi-l-qawli fa-yaṭmaʿa lladhī fī qalbihī maraḍun﴾

﴿then do not be complaisant in your speech, lest he in whose heart is a sickness should aspire﴾[409]

Therefore, it is extremely challenging to examine the differences between men and women thoroughly, and none of these differences indicate a man's superiority or closeness to God ﷻ.

In matters of politics, society, economy, and cultural development, the guidance of a jurist is required, as the consultation of the experts. However, the quality of its adaptation should be considered more religiously. This must be done without violating God's ﷻ decree or neglecting refined development. The goal is to ensure the protection of all divine laws while safeguarding women's happiness. Iran's support for it is inappropriate since the convention does not provide a practical way to achieve this

[408] Sūrat an-Nisā', Verse 11.

[409] Sūrat al-Aḥzāb, Verse 32.

balance. Merely implying conditions contrary to the spirit governing it has no credibility. Despite previous rejections in various legal contexts, the persistent push for its approval is perceived as an attempt to undermine the religious values that Sayyidah Fāṭimah ﷺ upholds.

Considering the moment when Amīr al-Mu'minīn ﷺ spoke to the Prophet ﷺ during the final moments of his beloved wife, stating,

> "Indeed, your daughter will inform you about how your community united to oppress her,"[410]

we encounter a parallel situation with certain individuals' approach to jurists and religious institutions, which purportedly promotes a unified environment.

Supporters of such a movement are caught between development and religion, leading them to alter religious principles to fit societal progression or introduce an illusory condition that does not appear to contradict Islāmic law. They face a dilemma of choosing between religion and development, or, God forbid, they fall prey to the enemy's deception, which, God willing, will never occur. If this is the case, this form of reformism is a spiritual ailment that can only be healed through divine intervention. The following verse illustrates such a disease:

---

[410] Sharīf Raḍī, Muḥammad b. al-Ḥusayn, *Nahj al-Balāghah*, Sermon 202.

﴿فَتَرَى الَّذِينَ فِي قُلُوبِهِم مَرَضٌ يُسارِعونَ فيهِم يَقولونَ نَخشىٰ أَن تُصيبَنا دائِرَةٌ ۚ فَعَسَى اللَّهُ أَن يَأتِيَ بِالفَتحِ أَو أَمرٍ مِن عِندِهِ فَيُصبِحوا عَلىٰ ما أَسَرّوا في أَنفُسِهِم نادِمينَ﴾

﴾*fa-tarā lladhīna fī qulūbihim maraḍun yusāri'ūna fīhim yaqūlūna nakhshā 'an tuṣībanā dā'iratun fa-'asā llāhu 'an ya'tiya bi-l-fatḥi 'aw 'amrin min 'indihī fa-yuṣbiḥū 'alā mā 'asarrū fī 'anfusihim nādimīna*﴿

﴾*Yet* you *see those in whose hearts is a sickness rushing to them, saying, 'We fear lest a turn of fortune should visit us.' Maybe God will bring about a victory, or a command from Him, and then they will be regretful for what they kept secret in their hearts,*﴿[411]

In other words, this heart is ill and hastily joins the group of religion-hating enemies and says as follows:

> "I fear that the situation will reverse and the non-believers will prevail."

God ﷻ will respond:

> "If there were a breakthrough or a new order, then the foreign enemies would be disgraced."

[411] Sūrat al-Mā'idah, Verse 52.

While the subject matter is broad, this provides a sufficient overview.

Āyatullāh 'Abd Allāh Jawādī Āmulī

July 2003

www.ingramcontent.com/pod-product-compliance
Lightning Source LLC
Chambersburg PA
CBHW051608120626
46551CBC0014B/1722
9781956276527